THE LATE BLOOMER'S GUIDE TO SUCCESS AT ANY AGE

SUSAN SULLY

Quill

An Imprint of HarperCollins*Publishers*

HarperCollins books may be purchased for educational, business, or sales promotional use. For information please write: Special Markets Department, HarperCollins Publishers Inc., 10 East 53rd Street, New York, NY 10022.

FIRST EDITION

Designed by Elliott Beard

Printed on acid-free paper

Library of Congress Cataloging-in-Publication Data has been applied for.

ISBN 0-380-81092-1

00 01 02 03 04 ❖/RRD 10 9 8 7 6 5 4 3 2 1

For late bloomers and their friends and teachers,
especially Marty Whaley Adams and Susan Virginia Hull

From **Song of the Open Road**

Afoot and light-hearted I take to the open road,
Healthy, free, the world before me,
The long brown path before me leading wherever I choose.

Henceforth I ask not good-fortune, I myself am good-fortune,
Henceforth I whimper no more, postpone no more, need
    nothing,
Done with indoor complaints, libraries, querulous criticisms,
Strong and content I travel the open road.

WALT WHITMAN, *Leaves of Grass*

Contents

PART THREE
Planning and Pursuing Life Change

Contents

Acknowledgments

Were it not for the contributions and assistance of many wonderful friends and colleagues—most of them late bloomers—this book would not exist in its present form. First thanks to my husband, Thomas Sully, for endlessly listening to my rantings, reveries, and written drafts and for encouraging me to write this book and to pursue my calling as a writer. Second thanks go to my agent, George Greenfield of Lecture Literary Management, whose tireless enthusiasm helped bring this books to press. Fervid and well-earned thanks to my dear companion and adviser in late-blooming life, Susan Hull, who helped me develop many of the ideas in this book and offered insightful and transforming commentary as an informal editor. Equally essential editorial advice was provided by Charles Cornwell of Lankin Cursley Company editorial services (lankincursley@bellsouth.net). Friend and shining example of the late-blooming life Marty Whaley Adams and budding late bloomer Cindy Hyder also provided important advice along the way. Thanks are also due to my official editors, Tia Maggini, whose expert advice shaped the final manuscript, and Clare

Hutton, whose enthusiasm for the book has been truly heart-warming.

I owe a deep debt of gratitude to all the late bloomers who agreed to be profiled in the book: Marty Whaley Adams (mwadams.com), John Carroll Doyle (johncdoyle.com), Nikki Hardin, editor of *Skirt!* (skirtmag.com), Cynthia Yacapraro of Café Cynthia, Peter Herman, Susan Hull, Jerri Chaplin, and the three who wished to remain anonymous. Thank you for sharing your inspiring examples with me and those who will read this book. With one exception, everyone profiled in this book lives and works in Charleston, South Carolina, which just proves that if you throw a rock (and make it a diamond, please), you'll probably hit a late bloomer—and a successful one at that.

I also wish to thank Diana Cohn for her friendship and for introducing me to George; Pamela Oline, therapist, mentor, and midwife of my second chance at life; and, in memoriam, Mary Vaughan, who taught me how to write and to break away from the crowd.

May you all bloom long and brightly.

Introduction

This is a book written for late bloomers by a late bloomer. It shouldn't surprise you to learn that I came up with the idea for this book more than ten years ago, but took a decade to get around to writing it—because I am a late bloomer. I desperately needed a book like this back then. But at that time there wasn't a single book out there for late bloomers. In fact, this is the only book I know of that specifically addresses our needs. It provides a comprehensive program of change that deals with the particular challenges—tangible and intangible, rational and utterly irrational—that we late bloomers contend with when we decide to rework our lives to more closely match the lives we've always dreamed of leading.

Fortunately, the ten years I spent not writing this book weren't wasted. In fact, as most late bloomers find out, time is rarely wasted. The experiences we gain, the self-knowledge we develop, and the skills we learn in jobs and walks of life that we may in the end abandon always bear fruit, one way or another. While secretly wishing with all my heart that I could be a full-time writer, I worked as an arts administrator. In particular, I specialized in strategic planning. My job was to help the staff and board members of arts organizations figure out what they wanted to do in the future, and how they were going to do it. Every so often, the irony of this situation would dawn on me, when I realized how much I, too, needed to get clear about what I was going to do with my own life.

As I look back over the first fifteen years of my adult life, I realize that I was slowly but surely working toward being who I am today: a full-time, self-supporting writer with several books to my name. Like most late bloomers, I had a lot to contend with. In addition to early struggles with depression, anxiety, and alcoholism, I also lived in a world in which writing wasn't thought of as a very good way to make a living. Every time I had the courage to describe the work I wanted to do, my dream was shot down. Sometimes the attack was obvious and deliberate: "There's no way you can make a living from writing." At other times, it came in the form of caring, yet pessimistic, sympathy: "You are choosing the hardest way in the world to make a living."

But one day I woke up from the bad dream I was living in. "There are plenty of people making a living from their writing," I told myself. "Why not me? Wouldn't it actually be easier for me to make a living doing something I love rather than by staying in a career that feels forced and uncomfortable? Anyway, what kind of a 'living' is that, when I don't even like what I do?"

From that day forward, I started questioning every bit of advice I received about my work and my life. I turned everything on its head. If someone told me not to push my luck when I was considering quitting a stable job to go out on my own as a freelancer, I said to myself, "Why *not* push my luck?" When I announced that my next book was going to be a bestseller, and someone told me not to count my chickens before they were hatched, I demanded to know, "Why not?" I had already discovered how much energy and joy I got from considering best-case scenarios. I wasn't about to stop counting my chickens—even if they weren't going to hatch.

This new attitude was a critical turning point in my life as a late bloomer. The other one came when my sister recommended that I apply the strategic planning techniques I had learned in my professional work to my own life as a would-be writer. Clearly, I should have thought of this myself but, as many late bloomers know, it often takes an outside opinion to get us really moving, so accustomed are we to ignoring our inner callings and cajolings. Once I actually started planning the way I was going to make changes in my life, and combined that strategic approach with the skeptical attitude I had developed toward conventional wisdom, the doors began to fly open in the career of my choice. There's no question that I had to work hard—perhaps harder than ever before—to move toward the life of my dreams. But the world seemed willing to meet me more than halfway once I got started.

It took me fifteen years to figure all this out, and another three years to reshape my life (aided by friends, teachers, and mentors) before I began to fulfill my dream of being a writer. With this book, I hope to help you shave five, ten, even fifteen years off the time it takes you to focus your energies upon your dreams and begin working toward them. In the following pages, I share the secret of my success: a combination of unconventional wisdom and practical planning techniques that addresses the complicated forces, both internal and external, that are probably holding you back. I use the stories of real-life late bloomers to illustrate my advice, so you can witness some of the ways that others have gone about changing their lives. And I offer a range of meditations, writing and planning exercises, and pursuits that are designed to involve you in an intense, revealing, and rewarding dialogue with yourself.

These activities will help you to draw upon your left-brain and your right-brain sources of intelligence: both rational thought and intuitive wisdom, observation and insight. By bringing all of these powers to the process of discerning your heart's desires and planning their pursuit, you can break free at last from the ties that hold you back. Like the great Houdini, you can perform a miraculous escape, casting off ropes and chains and locks, to burst into the bright light of your own exhilarating and fulfilling life.

If you are a late bloomer who is ready to think and act outside of the box, to stop surviving and start thriving, then this book is my gift to you. I hope that your transformation will be as thrilling and rewarding as mine was, and as were those of the other late bloomers described in these pages.

PART ONE

Getting Ready for Change

"How much longer must this charade go on?" I remember asking myself this question every morning as I put on clothes I didn't like, choked down a breakfast I could barely taste, and dashed out the door . . . late again for a job I could no longer stand. I would arrive at my desk, look at my list of things to do, and find myself unable to begin. I would drink coffee and stare out the window. And I would wonder, "What the hell is wrong with me?" I was perfectly capable of doing the work before me; I just couldn't bring myself to do it anymore. Deep down inside, I knew what I really wanted to be doing. But I couldn't figure out how on earth I was going to start making the changes I needed to make in order to do it.

Does this sound familiar? Is it getting harder and harder to show up for the work that you do, or the life that you live? Do you feel squelched desires, talents, or curiosities rising up inside of you and clamoring for attention? Maybe you feel like a split personality. There's that dutiful part of you that keeps showing up for the old life, the old work, the old way of being, and clings desperately to what it knows. And then there is that other part: the rebel inside of you, who grows more and more impatient with the status quo. This rebellious you spins elaborate fantasies of a new life that is filled with excitement, pleasure, and reward, while at the same time it sabotages your old life in subtle and not-so-subtle ways. Are you ready to give this part of you a chance, to listen to what it has to say, and let it lead you into a new life?

This book will engage you in an active dialogue with that rebellious self who is itching to break free, and with the timid one who keeps holding back. This dialogue will give you a chance to ask and answer vital questions about what you really want from life, and why. You may discover surprising things about yourself. And you *will* gain a clearer vision of the future that you have the power to create. By taking time to look within, you can orient yourself for change and tap into new sources of energy that will set you free from a life that no longer satisfies or nurtures you.

Start by answering the following questions as honestly as you can. Your answers will help you access that restless stirring inside, which, with proper attention and care, will burst into full bloom sooner rather than later.

1. Does it often feel like you are just going through the motions, with little in the way of excitement or fulfillment to show for it?

2. Does your current way of life or work seem to trigger bouts of depression or anxiety?

3. Do you have a burning desire to do something else?

4. Do you have a feeling that you haven't yet found your purpose in life, or that you haven't fully connected with life or work in a way that is energizing, inspiring, and fulfilling?

5. Do you feel thwarted, as if there is always some obstacle in your way which prevents you either from doing what you want to do or going where you want to go?

6. Are you afraid that you will never discover your true calling, or never find the courage to follow it?

7. Are you doing the work or living the life that you believe is right for you, but encountering a great deal of frustration or resistance along the way?

8. Do you often feel like an impostor, that you are pretending to be something or someone whom you know deep down inside you are not?

9. Do you suspect that there is a deep well of potential inside of you waiting to be tapped?

If you answered yes to any of these questions, then you are ready to begin your journey to a new way of living—one that is filled with purpose, excitement, and joy. The following chapters will help start you on your way.

CHAPTER 1

Why am I a late bloomer?

Recognizing a Pattern of
Frustration and Delay

What is a late bloomer?

I have met people in their late twenties who consider themselves to be late bloomers because they know they are
actively forging a path that is at odds with their inner callings,
settling for a life that falls far short of their dreams. I have
encountered people in their thirties, forties, and fifties who
appear successful but suspect in their hearts that they are late
bloomers because they want to achieve another, more personally meaningful form of success. I know people who have dedicated their adult lives to their most urgent callings, and yet are
still late bloomers because they have not found ways to translate

these callings into rewarding exchanges with the world. I have heard the stories of late bloomers who, having already bloomed once or even twice with great satisfaction, sense yet another flowering coming on in their sixties, seventies, and eighties.

If you are a late bloomer, you know it, even if others around you don't. Maybe you have the distinct conviction that there is another way of living, of working, or of expressing yourself that you have been putting off for a long time. Even though you may seem successful in the eyes of the world, you probably realize that you are no longer at peace with yourself or with your surroundings. Perhaps you feel that you aren't fulfilling the true potential of your unique gifts and talents, or that you are wasting time or throwing away opportunities. Maybe you suspect that there is a whole new life, and even a very different you, waiting just ahead, if only you could catch up and embrace it. And you probably find yourself wondering why you are standing still, instead of running ahead as fast as you can go.

Don't just make a living, create a life!

If you have allowed yourself to glimpse the way you want to live in the future, yet still find yourself clinging to an entirely different present, you are probably asking yourself, "What's holding me back?" A whole lot, is my answer. Clearly, many powerful factors can cause late bloomers to postpone the pursuit of happiness. Some of these have to do with popular misconceptions about work, life, and money. These misconceptions lure people into unsatisfying, unfulfilling situations early on in their lives and keep them there.

When people talk about making a living, they usually mean earning money. But a living is so much more than the balance of a bank account. Making a living is creating a life! When people talk about supporting themselves, they usually mean earning enough money to pay the bills. But how often do you think of supporting yourself emotionally, of nurturing your mind, body, and spirit with the activities that fill your waking hours?

In order to bloom fully and beautifully, it is important to put aside some of the common wisdom that we are taught by the conventional, materially obsessed world, and think unconventionally. Don't just make a living—create a life! Don't just support yourself—nurture your body and soul! Thomas Jefferson declared that the pursuit of happiness is one of our fundamental rights. Why should any of us settle for less? Unfortunately, the pressure to settle is strong. Why else would so many of us choose to follow unfruitful, unsatisfying pursuits?

Deciding too soon

In a way, the game is rigged against us from the start. In our late teens or early twenties, without much benefit of experience, we scramble for position in what feels like a life-or-death game of musical chairs. The music suddenly stops and we run for the nearest chair, which we then hold on to for dear life. Our parents and friends may urge us to finish school, get married, and start making a living. Fear of the unknown and a lack of faith in the abundance of the world send us lunging for the nearest college, job, or relationship. That same combination of fear and insufficient faith then works hard to keep us where we wound up, whether we like it there or not. We start to get rewards: perhaps financial success, social prominence, praise from employers, respect of co-workers and friends, a sense of security. Yet some of us find ourselves dying a little more each day as we betray our innermost dreams and desires.

There are, of course, late bloomers who suspect from the start that the game is rigged. They may simply decline to play at all, choosing instead to hover around the margins of life, working at odd jobs, toiling in obscurity, doing anything they can to avoid joining the throng of players who compete for dubious prizes. Unfortunately, refusal to play at all can be just as unsatisfying and unfruitful as playing by the rules.

The "Chorus of No"

Many of the forces that late bloomers contend with are irrational. They spring from deep-seated fears, beliefs, and programmed responses that limit your ability to perceive the full range of possibilities the world holds out to you. They are heard in the voices that tell you it is too late to start a new career, go back to school, or follow a calling that has been whispering to you for years. These are the fears that warn you that no one will like you if you do what you really want to do, say what you really think, and live life on your own terms, not anybody else's. These are the beliefs that insist you will fail even where others have succeeded, that you aren't as talented as you think, and that there is no room in the world for you to be who you really are.

Unfortunately, the world is full of naysayers, pessimists, and worrywarts who can be counted on to echo your fears and negative assumptions about yourself or about your life in general. I call these negative voices, both internal and external, the "Chorus of No." Like the toga-clad choruses in Greek tragedies, this group of pessimists warns the hero at every turn that he or she is about to make *A Big Mistake*. In order to bring about life change, we have to stop living our lives as if they are tragedies, fraught with irreversible errors that can only lead to misery and untimely, ignominious death. Why not see life as a comedy instead, full of laughter and surprise and the promise of a happy ending?

In classic comic literature, the Chorus of No is replaced by clowns, jesters, and fools. These characters, in their willingness to throw off the heavy garb of fear, assume a different kind of wisdom, the wisdom of happy children who are willing to take risks and make mistakes, then laugh at and learn from their experiences. Anyone who is familiar with the great comedies of Shakespeare and his ancient Greek predecessors knows that these plays offer as many life lessons as the tragedies do, and provide a lot more joy along the way.

Rewriting the rules

By reprogramming your heart and planning your future, you can change the way you live your life. Are you ready to break all the old rules and start playing by a whole new set that you create for yourself? Are you ready to choose the prizes you will work for? Are you ready to decide how you want to live, and achieve it, no matter what anyone else has to say about it? This may sound a bit overwhelming, but the ideas, exercises, and examples provided in this book will guide you through this process in gradual steps. In the following pages, you will find:

- *guided meditations* that limber up your mind, spark memories that can direct you back to your true self, tap unspoken self-knowledge and wisdom, and reshape your most limiting thoughts and beliefs;

- *writing exercises* that use the technique of speed-writing to help you to find out even more about yourself, until you discover the hidden truths, misconceptions, and fears that lie beneath the surface of your conscious mind;

- *Ten Principles of Unconventional Wisdom* that encourage you to break the old rules and defy expectations (others' and your own), and invite you to bloom brightly, proudly, and profusely;

- *planning exercises* that will help you to chart the course of action that will lead you out of dissatisfaction into the exhilarating pursuit of happiness;

- *pursuits* that describe specific ways in which you can practice breaking out of old patterns and start pursuing happiness right away; and

- *examples of late bloomers* whose stories reveal inspiring and innovative approaches to life change at any stage in the game.

If you are ready to envision the life you want to lead and start moving toward it now, then turn the page. Your future awaits.

CHAPTER 2

How do I want my life to be different?

Redefining Success

Do you really know what success means to you? We receive many messages about success from our family and friends, our peers, the marketplace, and society at large. When we were in school, success meant getting straight As, making the football team or cheerleading squad, or being elected class president. According to the popular media, success means driving a snazzy car, looking like a fashion model, having a gorgeous lover, raising two perfect children, making a lot of money, and enjoying the finer things in life. Success means impressing your boss. Success means earning the envy of those around you.

Success means doing something that your mother can brag about. But what about you? What does success mean to you?

Success is so commonly gauged by outside measurements that we are rarely, if ever, encouraged to find out what success really means to us. I remember being completely stumped when my mother asked me once, point-blank, "What do you really want from life?" I knew that I was miserably unhappy trying to fulfill everybody else's visions of success, but I had no idea of what really mattered to me. At the age of fifteen, I was a late bloomer-in-the-making. It took me another twenty years of testing myself against nearly every external standard of success that I could find before I finally realized that I had to define it for myself, from the inside out.

One of the most common reasons that late bloomers take the slow boat to happiness is that we choose, either consciously or not, to pursue someone else's definition of success. Consider this scenario. You work hard to get the degree, the job, the house, the lover, the car, the bonus, the sense of power, the one-week vacation, the sixty-hour workweek, the astronomical bills, the exhaustion, the sense of emptiness and longing, and a whopping need to escape. Not until you finally receive the fruits of your labor and find them less sweet than you imagined do you realize that you have been racing toward the wrong goalpost all along. Does this sound familiar?

Or, perhaps you find that you just can't get up a head of steam because the standards of success you are outwardly pursuing are not in sync with your internal values. You just can't bring yourself to work those extra overtime hours in order to win the bonus or the promotion. You can't be bothered to complete the course because you aren't really all that interested in the subject. You keep making lateral moves within the same career track, never getting above entry-level positions. You just don't care enough about the rewards (or the process) to apply your body, mind, and soul completely. You just paddle along, keeping your head above water, wondering when you will ever get ahead.

Or maybe you rebel. You decide you're not having any of it. You forge a completely alternative lifestyle. You decline the traditional rewards. You choose a life of spartan bohemianism (or footloose adventurism) that demonstrates the disdain you have for traditional values. And yet, somewhere along the line, you begin to suspect that you are shortchanging yourself. You begin to realize that you would like something more, or something different, in your life. Perhaps, you think, some of those rewards wouldn't be so bad, if only you could earn them on your own terms, and not be owned by them once you got them.

This is your chance to define the rewards that you want to get in your life. By now, you should have had enough experience to know the difference between what really matters to you and what only matters to other people. By creating a definition of success that truly excites you, that reflects your real values, and that fills you with desire and even impatience, you can reorient your whole life. You can describe in glowing terms the paradise toward which you will travel in this lifetime. This journey will probably be a long and challenging process. Most life changes are. But a clear idea of your destination and its desirability will help you get moving and keep moving toward it—full steam ahead.

If you are not satisfied with your current life or work, then you are probably operating with a definition of success that you have outgrown. In order to finally free yourself from it, you must become clear, right now, about what aspects of success you are ready to forego. You must also decide what kinds of success you will do just about anything to win from now on.

Consider Peter, a lawyer-turned-personal chef. At a certain point in his life, Peter realized that the money he was earning as a lawyer was no longer adequate payment for the things he was

19

giving up: leisure, time with his family, and his love of cooking. Once this became perfectly clear, it was much easier for him to give up a high-paying, respectable job and start all over again in a much lower-profile, lower-paying career. His new definition of success didn't include making a six-figure salary, having a job title his parents could brag about, or even owning a second car. At the top of his list was the joy of living a balanced life and doing work that brings pleasure to others, as well as to himself.

Like Peter, you must become as honest as possible about what you really value and let go of the value system you have outgrown. These decisions will most likely involve a loss of or decrease in rewards in certain areas, and may even spark concern and controversy among your circle of friends, family, and peers. But if you are clear with yourself about what you value and why, these decisions will be much easier to make, and you will find that your sense of energy is renewed and you can proceed enthusiastically as you change your life's course.

To become clearer about what you want to do in the next phase of your life, how you want to achieve it, and why, you need to consider many different elements of success. For the purposes of the following exercise, I will loosely describe these elements as *rewards*. One of the rewards our society values most is financial gain. But there are many other kinds of rewards that are equally valuable, or, for many people, even more so. These include a sense of meaning or accomplishment in life, and knowing that your work makes a positive contribution to the world. Another very rich reward is a sense of personal well-being, having the peace of mind and feelings of energy and enthusiasm that come when you are completely and joyfully engaged with life, in both work and leisure.

Good health is an essential reward, yet people sacrifice it all too often in the pursuit of other criteria of success. How many times have you skipped a meal, overindulged in alcohol, caffeine, sugar, or tobacco, or gone without exercise because you put other things first? Another measure of success is the way you are perceived and valued by others. All of us want to be valued and respected, but this way of measuring success can become quite dangerous if you place the desire to be approved or admired above other criteria of success that are more centered within your own sense of self.

A feeling of happiness and serenity is a measure of success that is not as elusive as some people would have us believe. The knowledge that you are actively merging your internal values and goals with the external order of your life is exhilarating, satisfying, and fulfilling. And what better definition of happiness is there than an exhilarating sense of satisfaction and fulfillment with your life? That is the kind of happiness we all want to pursue.

EXERCISES

The following exercises will help you to gain a better understanding of how you have been defining success and how you will define it from now on.

Exercise 1: How have I defined success?

1. Begin by tearing a piece of paper into twenty small strips just large enough to write a few words on (see the worksheet provided for this exercise at the end of this section).

2. Without thinking too much about what you are writing, or why, jot down a few words on each piece of paper that describe how you have defined success. The words you write down should complete this sentence: "I used to think success meant ___." Your answers might include:

"making my boss entirely dependent upon me," "having an impressive job title," or "making more money than my brother." Be completely honest with yourself and don't stop until you can't think of anything else to write. Look at the example provided if you need help getting started. If you need more than twenty pieces of paper to list all the elements that have made up your definition of success, then make as many as you need.

3. When you are done, organize these pieces of paper in order of the importance they have held for you. What has seemed absolutely essential to your sense of success? What has been very important to you? Somewhat important? To which elements have you only paid lip service, without really dedicating much time or effort to achieving them? Be honest with yourself and put these items last. Once you have finished arranging your pieces of paper in the order that reflects the priorities you are ready to leave behind, then create a written list of your old definition of success using the format suggested on the worksheet provided. (See the example for additional help.)

Exercise 1: How have I defined success?

Make two copies of this page, cut the copies along the lines into twenty small pieces, and complete the sentence printed on each piece of paper.

I used to think success meant _making my boss happy_	I used to think success meant _fulfilling other people's expectations_
I used to think success meant _being able to take fancy vacations_	I used to think success meant _having a job my mother and father were proud of_
I used to think success meant _not working more than 40 hours a week_	I used to think success meant _having a nice wardrobe_
I used to think success meant _knowing that there was a steady paycheck every month_	I used to think success meant _impressing people_
I used to think success meant _making enough money to eat out at nice restaurants_	I used to think success meant _looking and feeling healthy_

Exercise 1: How have I defined success?

Make two copies of this page, cut the copies along the lines into twenty small pieces, and complete the sentence printed on each piece of paper.

I used to think success meant	I used to think success meant
_____	_____
_____	_____
_____	_____
I used to think success meant	I used to think success meant
_____	_____
_____	_____
_____	_____
I used to think success meant	I used to think success meant
_____	_____
_____	_____
_____	_____
I used to think success meant	I used to think success meant
_____	_____
_____	_____
_____	_____
I used to think success meant	I used to think success meant
_____	_____
_____	_____
_____	_____

EXAMPLE

Exercise 1: How have I defined success?

Once you have organized your measures of success in order of importance, use the following format to create a list of these old priorities. Fill in the same words you wrote on the scraps of paper underneath the appropriate headings.

Elements that were essential to my past definition of success:
making my boss happy

fulfilling other people's expectations

impressing people

having a job my mother and father were proud of

Elements that were very important to my past definition of success:
knowing that there was a steady paycheck every month

being able to take fancy vacations

Elements that were somewhat important to my past definition of success:
having a nice wardrobe

making enough money to eat out at nice restaurants

Elements that were not really important to my past definition of success:
not working more than 40 hours a week (note: I always ended up working more)

looking and feeling healthy (note: I was always too unhappy and tired to work out)

WORKSHEET

Exercise 1: How have I defined success?

Once you have organized your measures of success in order of importance, use the following format to create a list of these old priorities. Fill in the same words you wrote on the scraps of paper underneath the appropriate headings.

Elements that were essential to my past definition of success:

Making everyone happy
Making my dependent on me
Not failing at anything
Helping everyone

Elements that were very important to my past definition of success:

Being liked by everyone
Acting happy all the time
Having alot of friends
Getting a College degree

Elements that were somewhat important to my past definition of success:

Being satisfied with w/I had
Working hard at the job
Being happy for others success
Making enough money for bills

Elements that were not really important to my past definition of success:

Wearing brand name clothes
Having my own car
Eating out all the time
Living high on the hog.

Exercise 2: How do I plan to define success from now on?

1. Tear up twenty more strips of paper (see the worksheet provided for this exercise). This time, write a few words on each piece of paper that complete this sentence: "I will feel successful when ___." Describe all the elements that you think will really make you feel successful, fulfilled, and happy. These should include tangible, spiritual, and emotional rewards, such as: "I am able to buy a house," "I don't need to smoke any more," "I know that I am sharing the talents God gave me with others," or "I no longer feel a sense of emptiness at the end of the day." They should range from the profound to the banal, and include things you are proud to admit about yourself and things you might not want to share with anyone else. Take a look at the examples provided if you need more help getting started.

2. *Optional:* If you are one of those people who work better with images than with words, or if you just want to experiment more with this exercise, you can sit down with a pile of old magazines, newspapers, and catalogues and flip through them, cutting out any pictures or words that attract your attention as you think about success. When you are done, tear up as many strips of paper as you have clippings, and write on each strip a few words that translate the images or words you have clipped into descriptions of rewards that will contribute to your sense of success.

3. Now, organize your new pieces of paper in order of their importance to you, starting with the elements that are absolutely essential to promoting a sense of success and happiness in the life you want to lead, and ending with those that are least important. Keep moving the pieces around until the order feels correct. If something you wrote down seems out of

place, perhaps representing an old value that you no longer hold or that you wish to leave behind, put it last.

4. When you are done, write down your new definition of success using the format suggested on the worksheet provided. Look at the example if you need a little more help prioritizing your new definition of success. Is your new definition surprising? Did you discover anything new about yourself and what you value? Does this new definition of success differ significantly from the way you have been defining success up until now? Are you ready to let go of some of the old elements you described in reply to the first exercise and work hard to achieve these new ones? If you are a late bloomer, my guess is that your answer to all these questions is "Yes!"

Exercise 2: How do I plan to define success from now on?

Make two copies of this page, cut the copies along the lines into twenty small pieces, and complete the sentence printed on each piece of paper.

I will feel successful when I love the work I do	I will feel successful when I feel centered and energized
I will feel successful when I am answering my creative calling daily by making art	I will feel successful when my artwork is admired and collected by people I respect
I will feel successful when I get paid well to do work I love	I will feel successful when I have proven that I can make a living on my own terms
I will feel successful when I have the energy and self- respect to take care of my body	I will feel successful when I have a nice wardrobe that reflects my personality
I will feel successful when I have a beautiful home that reflects my values and interests	I will feel successful when I have friends who share my values and encourage and inspire me

WORKSHEET

Exercise 2: How do I plan to define success from now on?

Make two copies of this page, cut the copies along the lines into twenty small pieces, and complete the sentence printed on each piece of paper.

I will feel successful when _I become the person God meant for me to be_	I will feel successful when _I write a book_
I will feel successful when _I own my own home._	I will feel successful when _I have a job that I love_
I will feel successful when _I get paid to do what I love._	I will feel successful when _I don't need the patch in order to not smoke_
I will feel successful when _I have a nice wardrobe._	I will feel successful when _I am contributing to the finances_
I will feel successful when _I am respected by others_	I will feel successful when _When I can truly have an intimate relationship with my husban_

EXAMPLE

Exercise 2: How do I plan to define success from now on?

Once you have organized your new definitions of success in order of importance, use the following format to create a list of these new priorities. Fill in the same words you wrote on the scraps of paper underneath the appropriate headings.

Elements that are essential to my new definition of success:

<u>I love the work I do</u>

<u>I feel centered and energized</u>

<u>I am answering my creative calling daily by making art</u>

<u>I have the energy and self-respect to take care of my body</u>

<u>I have friends who share my values and encourage and inspire me</u>

Elements that are very important to my new definition of success:

<u>my artwork is admired and collected by people I respect</u>

<u>I get paid well to do work I love</u>

<u>I have proven that I can make a living on my own terms</u>

<u>I have a beautiful home that reflects my values and interests</u>

Elements that are somewhat important to my definition of success:

<u>I have a nice wardrobe that reflects my personality</u>

Elements that are not really important to my new definition of success:

<u>my mother and father approve of my work</u>

31

WORKSHEET

Exercise 2: How do I plan to define success from now on?

Once you have organized your new definitions of success in order of importance, use the following format to create a list of these new priorities. Fill in the same words you wrote on the scraps of paper underneath the appropriate headings.

Elements that are essential to my new definition of success:

Becoming the person God made
Having a job that I love
Being able to converse in Spanish
Writing a book

Elements that are very important to my new definition of success:

Owning a home
Quit smoking
Having a nice wardrobe

Elements that are somewhat important to my new definition of success:

Getting into shape
Making good money
Getting respect
Helping my husband w/ bills

Elements that are not really important to my new definition of success:

Having alot of friends

CHAPTER 3

Where do I want to go?

Envisioning a Better Future

I am not the betting type, but I am willing to wager that any-one reading this book has entertained the fantasy of being interviewed for an article or a television talk show about him- or herself at least once. "Tell me about the challenges you had to overcome to achieve success," says the interviewer. "What is the most important thing in your life today?" inquires the talk show host. If you are exceedingly modest even in your private fantasies, maybe this imaginary conversation just takes place between you and a close friend. "Tell me how you did it," prompts the friend, wanting to know how you succeeded in breaking free from fear and expectation to change your life, once and for all.

If you haven't ever dared to describe the life you want to lead to yourself or to that hypothetical interviewer, I want to invite you to do so now. Most good strategic planning programs for individuals and organizations include what is called *vision work*: envisioning the new way things will be, once the planning and execution of the plan are done. It is understood that this vision will evolve, both during the planning process and through the implementation of the plan. But a planning process must begin with a general idea of where it is leading. Once your vision for the future is at least partially clear, you can measure the gap between where you are and where you want to be, and describe the step-by-step goals and actions needed to lead you where you want to go.

For some late bloomers, this destination will be fairly clear: going back to school to become a lawyer, giving up a law practice to pursue a creative career, giving up a career to adopt a child and become a late-blooming mother. But if you are one of those late bloomers who have not yet gained clarity about where you would like to go in the next stage of your life, don't worry. Plenty of late bloomers start their process of transformation informed by nothing more certain than the knowledge that they need to make a change. If you were able to complete the previous exercise about defining success, then you have enough information to start planning. The rest will become clear as you go along.

If you cannot yet describe a clear, concrete vision for your future, I suggest that you develop a vision of how you would like to change your life in the coming year. This vision may simply involve making minor adjustments to your current life, with the goal of bringing it into closer alignment with your real values. Small actions can trigger major internal shifts that can clarify your vision for the future. When you are ready, you can begin to work toward that vision. In the meantime, just begin by planning small adjustments to your current way of life.

Maybe this means devoting thirty minutes a day to a burning interest that might develop into a whole new career direction. Perhaps it means letting go of a particular commitment that is no longer rewarding or exciting. One late bloomer I know began her transformation by going to Weight Watchers to change her eating habits. Before long, she was considering changing her career completely in order to start a low-fat, gourmet catering service.

Another late bloomer I met had two competing visions for her future. The first involved adjusting her existing career in a way that would allow her greater creative expression and freedom within that field. The second called for a total change of direction, and for starting over again in a completely different field. The first sounded more sensible; the second, more outlandish. Yet after she considered how she really wanted to experience success, and what rewards would contribute the most fulfillment and excitement to her life, she chose this second, more radical path.

The most common mistake late bloomers can make at this point is to try to keep several visions alive and active at once. Choose a vision that has the greatest attraction for you now, and plan for and live with that vision for the next three months. If, at the end of that time, you feel strongly that you have selected the wrong destination, then you can begin your process again, informed by personal experience. Trial and error is the only way that you can truly discover what works and what doesn't work for you. By planning and setting out on a gradual course of change, you can make progress without jeopardizing your well-being.

Finally, a word to the late bloomer who has a clear sense of direction. Take a moment to be grateful for your clarity. Not everyone is so blessed. But don't be tempted to skip the following exercises. Just because you have a clear sense of where you want to be in a few years' time does not mean that you won't encounter challenges and obstacles along the way. You need to spend time fleshing out your vision for the future in order to ensure that it won't turn into a mirage that shimmers and shines just a few miles ahead, failing to materialize in this life. If you purposefully invoke your vision for the future as a tangible, achievable reality, you will begin to take it seriously as a genuine destination instead of dismissing it as an unattainable, unrealistic fantasy. By harnessing your imagination to envision the future as clearly as possible, you can take one giant step forward in transforming that elusive mirage into reality.

EXERCISES

Exercise 1: Envisioning your future

Find a quiet time when you can sit in a comfortable place, uninterrupted by telephone calls or visitors, and interview yourself using the following questions. The purpose of this exercise is to think freely, confidently, and excitedly about your future. It will probably be helpful to ask that chorus of voices inside your head that says "No!" to your every inner desire to sit outside the room or, even better, to go on a long and involved errand somewhere. Members of that chorus won't be needed here. If one or two of them do pop their heads into the room, remind them that this is a private interview.

Imagine that this interview is taking place three years from now. (If you have trouble with this time frame, you can shorten it to one year or lengthen it to five.) Imagine that you have already succeeded in changing your life and are enjoying the fruits of your labor. You are a smashing success in the way you have always dreamt of, and you want to share the good news with others so that they will know more about you and your successful strategies, and perhaps will find the courage to follow your example. Finally, decide who your interviewer is. Is it a journalist from one of your favorite magazines, or a television talk show host? Perhaps it is a close friend with whom you share the details of your life. Maybe it's someone who is no longer in this world, a deceased friend or family member who always wanted what was best for *you,* not for everyone else. Or maybe it's that genial voice inside of you that urges you on when everyone else tells you to stop.

Imagine your interviewer sitting next to you while you answer the questions he or she asks. You may want to answer by speaking out loud. Or you can answer silently in your head, or you may prefer to write down your replies. However you use this interview, be sure to make a written record of your responses at some point (see the example and worksheet provided at the end of this section for a helpful format). You will refer to them later.

1. Describe a day in your life. *(Remember: This interview is taking place one to five years from now. Answer this and the remaining questions as if you are already living in the future.)* With what specific activities do you pursue your interests and use your gifts? How do you spend your time?

2. "To thine own self be true" is great advice for late bloomers. You are a wonderful example of how following this advice can lead to a life that is exciting to live and inspiring to observe. How has being true to yourself shaped the life you lead today?

3. Clearly, a life lived this way is a great gift, to you and to others. What are some of the benefits you receive from following your heart's desire? How does the world benefit from your life and work?

4. Are there any sacrifices that you make to live this life? Why are you willing to make these sacrifices?

5. What would you say is the single most important thing you do?

6. What are the biggest differences between the life you led three *(or one or five)* years ago and your life today?

7. What were the biggest challenges you had to address in order to get to where you are now? How did you overcome them?

8. Clearly, something fueled you on during this process. What gave you the energy you needed to make these changes?

9. Do you have any words of advice for others who want to change their lives and be true to themselves?

EXAMPLE

Exercise 1: Envisioning your future

Answering as if you were responding to interview questions posed three years from now (or however many years you are comfortable planning ahead), write short but detailed replies to the following questions.

1. Describe a day in your life. With what specific activities do you pursue your interests and use your gifts? How do you spend your time?

   I wake up full of energy and enthusiasm for the day ahead. I spend part of the workday completing commissions for paintings that clients are waiting for and dealing with the business of my art career: planning exhibitions, updating my mailing list, etc.; the rest of the day, I plan new paintings, observe the world, fuel my artistic engines. On weekends, I spend time with my family and enjoy hobbies like gardening and sailing.

2. "To thine own self be true" is great advice for late bloomers. You are a wonderful example of how following this advice can lead to a life that is exciting to live and inspiring to observe. How has being true to yourself shaped the life you lead today?

   First, I had to start listening to the voice inside my heart that insisted I honor my calling as an artist. Then, I had to learn to ignore the voice that said I had to fulfill other people's expectations. I also had to ignore external voices that said I couldn't make a living as an artist. Once I put my trust in my own inner voice, I found that I could find a path and follow it.

3. Clearly, a life lived this way is a great gift, to you and to others. What are some of the benefits you receive from following your heart's desire? How does the world benefit from your life and work?

   <u>I used to feel a separation between work and life. Work was</u>
   <u>something unpleasant that I had to do in order to make enough</u>
   <u>money to live. But by the time I got around to "living," I was too</u>
   <u>exhausted and angry to enjoy life. Now work is something I love</u>
   <u>to do—it is one of the most rewarding aspects of my life. I trans-</u>
   <u>late and share that joy through my work with those who see it, as</u>
   <u>well as with those people I share my life with.</u>

4. Are there any sacrifices that you make to live this life? Why are you willing to make these sacrifices?

   <u>For several years, my income dipped significantly. My family</u>
   <u>felt the effect of this, but I was so much happier, such a better</u>
   <u>person to be around, that they didn't mind. Now, I feel that I am a</u>
   <u>much better example to my children than I was before when I was</u>
   <u>overworked, frustrated, exhausted, and angry all the time.</u>

5. What would you say is the single most important thing you do?

   <u>Being authentic every single day. Being true to myself. For me,</u>
   <u>this means expressing my true talents and calling through my</u>
   <u>daily work—and practicing a daily faith that reminds me that there</u>
   <u>are rewards for doing this—emotional, spiritual, AND material.</u>

6. What are the biggest differences between the life you led three *(or one or five)* years ago and your life today?

I love the work I do. I no longer feel like I am wasting my life. I feel like a success, even though I don't make any more money than I used to. The praise I get from others really means something to me because I am proud of the work I do. I feel totally and joyfully engaged with life.

7. What were the biggest challenges you had to address in order to get to where you are now? How did you overcome them?

I had to learn to deal with fear of the unknown and anxiety. I knew how to make a living as a real estate agent; I had no idea how to make a living as an artist. I had to believe that I could do it, then be willing to put in the time to learn how to do it and keep moving forward, despite all the fear I felt. I also had to learn to put myself first in my life.

8. Clearly, something fueled you on during this process. What gave you the energy you needed to make these changes?

Desperation! I couldn't live my life any longer the way I was. My health was suffering—I was smoking, overeating, not exercising, getting depressed. I knew that life had to have something more to offer. Wanting to escape the pain I was in was the biggest motivating force; that, and this nagging voice inside that kept trying to tell me I was ignoring my true calling.

9. Do you have any words of advice for others who want to change their lives and be true to themselves?

Remember that Rome was not built in a day. It took years to create the life that is making you unhappy. Strong forces and fears encourage you to live this way. You have to be willing to devote several years to creating a new life, and you have to put cotton in your ears and ignore the bad advice that shaped your old life. Learn to listen to yourself, and be willing to work hard for what you want!

Exercise 1: Envisioning your future

Answering as if you were responding to interview questions posed three years from now (or however many years you are comfortable planning ahead), write short but detailed replies to the following questions.

1. Describe a day in your life. With what specific activities do you pursue your interests and use your gifts? How do you spend your time?

_____

_____

_____

_____

_____

_____

_____

2. "To thine own self be true" is great advice for late bloomers. You are a wonderful example of how following this advice can lead to a life that is exciting to live and inspiring to observe. How has being true to yourself shaped the life you lead today?

_____

_____

_____

_____

_____

_____

_____

3. Clearly, a life lived this way is a great gift, to you, and to others. What are some of the benefits you receive from following your heart's desire? How does the world benefit from your life and work?

_____

_____

_____

_____

_____

_____

_____

4. Are there any sacrifices that you make to live this life? Why are you willing to make these sacrifices?

_____

_____

_____

_____

_____

_____

_____

5. What would you say is the single most important thing you do?

_____

_____

_____

_____

_____

_____

_____

6. What are the biggest differences between the life you led three *(or one or five)* years ago and your life today?

_____

_____

_____

_____

_____

_____

_____

7. What were the biggest challenges you had to address in order to get to where you are now? How did you overcome them?

_____

_____

_____

_____

_____

_____

_____

8. Clearly, something fueled you on during this process. What gave you the energy you needed to make these changes?

_____

_____

_____

_____

_____

_____

_____

9. Do you have any words of advice for others who want to change their lives and be true to themselves?

_____

_____

_____

_____

_____

_____

_____

Exercise 2: Creating a "vision statement"

Once you have completed the above exercise, you will be ready to write a "vision statement"—the first piece of your plan for life change. A vision statement is a concise description of the state you want to achieve for yourself. It can be as short as a paragraph, or as long as a page or more if you go into details. Your vision statement should address the following issues simply and directly. The answers you wrote to questions one through five in the previous interview exercise will include a good deal of this information. See the worksheets and examples provided for more help completing your vision statement.

1. What will the focus of your new life be? To what activity(ies), goal(s), or purpose(s) will you direct significant amounts of your time and talents?

2. How will this new focus reward and sustain you? How will it benefit others?

3. What changed physical, emotional, or mental states will accompany your dedication to this new focus?

4. How will this fulfill the new definition of success that you created in chapter 2?

For example, someone who wishes to become a freelance caterer might organize his replies into a vision statement like this one:

I will use my cooking talent and my ability to prepare and present delicious, beautiful, and healthful food to run a small catering business. I will specialize in creating imaginative table settings and surprising presentations of food that will delight and satisfy my clients. The combination of my entrepreneurial instincts and my culinary skills will result in a successful business that will be rewarding and satisfying to me as well as to my clients. I will enjoy the adrenaline rush of "putting on the show" during jobs, as well as the more creative, reflective pleasures of planning meals and presentations. My business-oriented side will enjoy the challenge of marketing my services to new clients.

A future writer might create a vision statement like the following:

I will become a full-time writer who makes a living from my writing. I will specialize in the areas of sports and travel, matching my own interests to those popular with the reading public to create a lucrative career. I will enjoy learning more about these fields of interest, I will get a satisfying feeling knowing that others are reading my work, and I will feel further rewarded by receiving a check at the end of the job. I will no longer waste my time and energy in unrelated jobs that take me away from the work I am meant to do and, when I am no longer so frustrated, I will be healthier and less tempted by self-destructive habits.

When you have finished writing your vision statement, put it in a safe place. This statement will appear at the top of your plan for life change—and it will inspire you during both the planning process and the implementation of your plan. If you are not anxious about letting others read your vision statement, then put it in a prominent location, like on the door of your refrigerator or in the corner of a mirror you use daily. Read it every day to remind yourself of the destination toward which you are traveling. If you'd rather keep your vision statement to yourself, then place it somewhere more private. Tape it to the front page of your journal or the inside of your closet door. Wherever you place your vision statement, just don't lose sight of it. It has the power to lead you to greater success and happiness as long as you keep it foremost in your mind.

EXAMPLE

Exercise 2: Creating a vision statement

Write a brief but detailed vision statement that describes the life you want to live and the work you want to do within one to five years. Be sure to include some of the thoughts from the previous exercise. Your vision statement should directly address the following questions. You may want to answer these first, then put your answers together into a paragraph or two (see the following example and worksheet).

1. What will the focus of your new life be? To what activity(ies), goal(s), or purpose(s) will you direct significant amounts of your time and talents?

   My artwork: improving my technical skills as a painter; learning more about the business side of the art field; creating a body of work that is collectible; observing the world and translating what I perceive into paintings that are beautiful and meaningful. My family: spending more quality time with my spouse and children. Leisure activities: more time gardening, exercising, relaxing with friends.

2. How will this new focus reward and sustain you? How will it benefit others?

   Even if I still have to work part-time as a realtor for a while, I will know that I am finally answering my calling. The artwork will be its own reward in many ways. I will love getting paid to paint—selling paintings will help disprove a very damaging belief I had that no one valued what I valued most highly about myself. Others will enjoy my paintings. My family and friends will enjoy this new, happier me.

3. What changed physical, emotional, or mental states will accompany your dedication to this new focus?

   I will be less drawn to unhealthy physical behavior when I am _happier. I will feel much more connected to and fulfilled by the_ _work I do. I will have more energy and enthusiasm for life. I may_ _make less money for a few years, maybe even permanently, but_ _will find ways to make ends meet and enjoy the other benefits of_ _my new work._

4. How will this fulfill the new definition of success that you created in chapter 2?

   I will love the work I do. I'll be centered and energized. I'll be _answering my calling. Even if I can't afford major new home_ _improvements, I will use my artwork to beautify my home. Wearing_ _jeans to work will actually reflect my personality better than the_ _expensive, uncomfortable clothes I used to wear to the office._

WORKSHEET

Exercise 2: Creating a vision statement

Write a brief but detailed vision statement that describes the life you want to live and the work you want to do within one to five years. Be sure to include some of the thoughts from the previous exercise. Your vision statement should directly address the following questions. You may want to answer these first, then put your answers together into a paragraph or two (see the following example and worksheet).

1. What will the focus of your new life be? To what activity(ies), goal(s), or purpose(s) will you direct significant amounts of your time and talents?

_____
_____
_____
_____
_____
_____
_____

2. How will this new focus reward and sustain you? How will it benefit others?

_____
_____
_____
_____
_____
_____
_____

3. What changed physical, emotional, or mental states will accompany your dedication to this new focus?

_____

_____

_____

_____

_____

_____

_____

4. How will this fulfill the new definition of success that you created in chapter 2?

_____

_____

_____

_____

_____

_____

_____

My Vision Statement

I will dedicate my life to my painting. I will make sure that making art plays a role in my everyday life, whether by actually working in my studio, reading about art, thinking about paintings, taking classes, going to galleries and museums, etc. As long as necessary, I will continue to work as a realtor, but I will negotiate a deal with my boss that will allow me more flexible hours to provide regular time for painting. I will learn how to sell my paintings, and work hard until income from painting supports my basic needs and those of my family. Ultimately, I will give up selling real estate for good.

Even though I may be putting in longer hours for less pay for a while, I will be fueled by the knowledge that I am finally answering my calling. People will begin to recognize my hidden talents; I will stop feeling like an impostor. I will feel a new level of joy and authenticity that will be expressed through my work and my daily life. I will no longer feel the need to "feed" my dissatisfaction by smoking and overeating. I will want to take care of my body so that I have energy to do the work that excites me. I will also make sure to have time for activities like gardening and being with friends and family that nurture and relax me.

My Vision Statement

_____

_____

_____

_____

_____

_____

_____

_____

_____

_____

_____

_____

_____

_____

_____

_____

_____

_____

_____

_____

_____

_____

_____

_____

_____

_____

_____

_____

_____

_____

_____

Pursuit: Living your vision

The purpose of this pursuit is to translate your vision for the future into immediate reality, both to prove that what you want to do is not as farfetched as it seems and also to remind you of the immediate rewards that await you. Before actually becoming a professional writer, I began practicing activities that allowed me to feel like one. For example, I researched numerous hypothetical articles. I conducted interviews, collected information, and researched topics at the library. As I did so, I felt a surge of excitement and well-being. It felt right. The hours flew by and I had fun. And surprisingly (to me), people took me seriously. They wanted to know what magazine I was working for. They assumed that I actually *was* a writer. They believed in me even though I wasn't sure I believed in myself. These experiences gave me a foundation upon which to build a future as a writer. They reinforced my conviction that this was the right vision for me, and they showed me that if I worked hard enough, I could transform this vision into the substance of my life.

Reread the thoughts you recorded during the last exercise and try to identify something that you can do in the very near future that will allow you to experience your vision as a reality for a few hours, a day, or even a whole weekend. For example, if your vision is to be a dance therapist, then you could volunteer to assist a professional dance therapist during a session. If you want to be a lawyer, you can intern in a friend's office for several afternoons or observe a trial. If your vision is to be a travel writer, take a little trip (in your own town or somewhere else) and write an article about it as if you really were on assignment. Whatever it is, get ready and do it! The following worksheets will help you get started.

While you are living your dream, pay full attention to the

rewards you experience. What gives you pleasure? What engages your curiosity or your talents? What new talents do you discover? How do people respond to you? Does time seem to pass differently? What is your energy level like? Are you calmer, more excited, or just plain happier than usual?

EXAMPLE

Pursuit: Living your vision

Describe a way you might be able to experience your vision as a reality for a few hours, a day, or even a whole weekend in the near future:

I could take a personal day and start making a painting of one of the beautiful old houses I am currently trying to sell for the real estate company. Just spending a day painting would be a step forward in proving to myself that I can do this. And if the painting turns out well, I might even be able to sell it to the person who eventually buys the house, or the person who is selling it! I will be killing two birds with one stone—getting started painting and thinking about creative ways to sell my artwork!

List the actions you need to take to make this happen, then check them off as you complete them:

Actions	Done
Schedule a personal day	
Get my painting supplies	
Choose a house to paint	
_Do it!_	

When you have completed this pursuit, briefly answer the following questions:

What gave you pleasure as you followed this pursuit?
I reconnected with my love of painting—I loved everything about doing it! I also loved the feeling of not going to the office.

What new talents did you discover?
I really am a good painter! And I have good ideas about selling my work!

How did people respond to you?

My boss didn't have a problem with me taking a personal day.
People who saw me painting on the street were impressed and
assumed I was a full-time painter. My family was excited to see
me so enthusiastic about something!

Did time seem to pass differently?

It flew! I want to do it again, and soon!

What was your energy level like? Were you calmer, more
excited, or just plain happier than usual?

I felt a whole new kind of energy flowing through me—I lost
track of time, like I was in a trance, then I felt exhilarated. It was
great!!!

Pursuit: Living your vision

Describe a way you might be able to experience your vision as a reality for a few hours, a day, or even a whole weekend in the near future:

_____

_____

_____

_____

_____

_____

_____

_____

List the actions you need to take to make this happen, then check them off as you complete them:

Actions   Done

_____   _____

_____   _____

_____   _____

_____   _____

When you have completed this pursuit, briefly answer the following questions:

What gave you pleasure as you followed this pursuit?

_____

_____

_____

What new talents did you discover?

_____

_____

How did people respond to you?

_____

_____

_____

_____

Did time seem to pass differently?

_____

_____

_____

_____

What was your energy level like? Were you calmer, more excited, or just plain happier than usual?

_____

_____

_____

_____

Getting ready for change

Now that you have completed these exercises and the pursuit, and allowed yourself to envision the future you want to live and even to experience it for a moment or two, you are probably ready to start making real changes. Yet how many times in the past have you boldly set out to change your life, only to find yourself turning back? Perhaps fears assailed you, or anxiety disabled you, or small words of discouragement or even well-meaning but misplaced concern from friends and family members immobilized you. You stood poised on the brink of transformation, but felt like you were sinking into quicksand. Even when you were fully aware of the steps you needed to take to change your life, you could not muster the courage you needed to move ahead.

Certainly, a well-thought-out plan can help you to identify the steps you need to take. The process of writing this plan is spelled out in part 3 of this book. Interactive exercises and examples will help you to describe an achievable plan for change that will direct your transformation. But no plan alone, however thoughtful and thorough it is, can get you from here to there by itself. You will also have to find a whole new belief system to support your plan before you can successfully take the actions that will transform your life. I know, because I have made more than one false start myself and ended up scurrying back to old ways of being because I wasn't ready to let go of the fears and misconceptions that were holding me back. In fact, you will need to adopt this new system of belief before you can even *begin* to plan your future. If you don't, your plan will be too modest and too filled with compromise. It will be doomed to fall short of its mark.

You must adopt a whole new way of thinking, one that is filled with courage, inspiration, and the spirit of irreverence, in order to overcome the fear and inertia that hold you back. The following chapters describe a new set of principles for late bloomers to live by. These principles defy conventional wisdom, offering unexpected and liberating inversions of traditional advice which invite you to think—and act—in unconventional and unfamiliar ways. Are you ready to challenge the fears and anxieties sung by the Chorus of No? Are you ready to believe that life is full of unexpected joy and happy endings, and act that way? Are you ready to live and work joyfully and creatively?

If you are, then prepare to enter a whole new world of possibility.

PART TWO

Ten Principles of Unconventional Wisdom

Welcome to the world of infinite potential—a world in which dreams come true, fantasies find fulfillment, and even unspoken desires are satisfied. Unfortunately, most of us spend too little time in this wonderful world, living instead in a far more narrow realm in which we are encouraged to follow careful lives, satisfy only small expectations, demand little, worry often, and avoid risk and change. This limiting realm is a dictatorship that derives its power from the principle of fear: fear of failure, fear of success, fear of abandonment, fear of self, fear of death, and, ultimately, fear of life. As long as you let these fears have power over you, you will remain obedient to the principles of this dictatorship.

Perhaps this sounds melodramatic. It can't be that bad, you may be thinking. But if you are reading this book, you must have admitted to yourself that you *are* a late bloomer. And if you have read this far, you have probably gained greater insights into some of the forces that have kept you from finding the satisfaction you want in this life. Just stop for a moment and recall how people have reacted when you have described your fantasy of a happy, fulfilling life. I hope you have found a few loving friends or adventurous souls who have commended and encouraged you. But I am sure you have encountered many more people who have responded at best with shocked disbelief and at worst with dire warnings of the many dangers that await you if you choose to travel this new path.

If you stop to consider the following words of advice, which have been uttered so frequently and fervently in our society that they have taken on the weight of proverbs, you will realize how fear controls the world of limited possibility:

Look before you leap.

Don't bite off more than you can chew.

Don't count your chickens before they're hatched.

Don't put all your eggs in one basket.

Look out for the danger signals.

Quit while you're still ahead.

Don't push your luck.

These words of traditional wisdom counsel caution, restraint, and compromise. But in the world of infinite possibility, we can toss these proverbs out and find a new way of living that celebrates creativity and uncompromising authenticity while accepting loss, sacrifice, and even occasional failure as inevitable parts of a well-lived life. In this brave new world, alternative rules turn the old ones upside down:

Leap before you look.

Bite off more than you can chew.

Count your chickens before they're hatched.

Put all your eggs in one basket.

Ignore the danger signals.

Don't quit while you're ahead.

Push your luck.

By inverting conventional wisdom, these principles invite you to adopt an attitude of far-reaching ambition, courageous risk-taking, and uncompromising individuality. To these I've added a few more principles to speed you on your way to the success you have only allowed yourself to dream of in the past:

"Honor yourself." Stop worrying so much about what others want and expect from you—be they your mother and father, sister or brother, life partner, friends, employers, or clients—and get clear about who *you* are, what *you* want, and what *you* plan to do about it. This principle focuses upon self-knowledge, self-love, and self-respect—true taboos in the realm of limited possibility.

"Believe and you will see." This challenges the conventional credo of faithlessness: "I'll believe it when I see it." If we must see first in order to believe, then how can we create, or feel mystery, or have hope or faith? Faith, and the sense of permission it nurtures, is essential to creative, joyful living. It is your companion through risk, your solace during failure, and your source of strength and courage during bursts of achievement.

And finally, "Just say 'Yes!'" Throw negativity out the window once and for all. Give yourself permission to live, to experiment, to enjoy, and to succeed. Say "Yes!" to your calling, your dreams, and the world that embraces you.

The following chapters present the Ten Principles of Unconventional Wisdom that rule this new world of infinite potential. In this world, fear is replaced with faith, obedience with irreverence, worry with permission, passiveness with proactiveness, and bare survival with creative living. This is a world in which late bloomers can send their roots down deep into fertile soil and find sustenance, a world in which new growth will shoot up and find the sun, and new flowers will break forth in shapes, sizes, colors, and scents that defy expectation and offer endless delight.

By working through the exercises provided in the following chapters and practicing the pursuits described in these pages, you will clear a path into this paradise of potential and lay the foundation upon which you will build your new life. Now, prepare the way for change.

CHAPTER 4

First Principle of Unconventional Wisdom

Honor Yourself

During a workshop for late bloomers, I invited the participants to consider the word "self-centeredness." I told them to consider "self-centeredness" as a healthy state of being essential to fruitful living, and then asked them to describe what thoughts and feelings emerged when they tried to apply this interpretation to themselves. A long and pregnant pause followed. Finally, one of the participants reacted.

"You can call a woman just about any bad name in the dictionary and she can deal with it," she exclaimed. "But call her self-centered and you hit her below the belt." Waves of agreement rippled through the room as each participant offered his or her own negative reaction to the word "self-centeredness." The intense resistance this diverse group of men and women encountered in attempting to adopt an attitude of self-centeredness is not surprising, considering the fact that the group was comprised of late bloomers. I dread to think how they might have reacted if I had asked them to imagine "having a high opinion of oneself."

Many late bloomers have a hard time putting themselves first in their lives. Perhaps this is because so many of us suffer from low self-esteem, are perennial people-pleasers, or have grown accustomed to measuring and judging ourselves by other people's standards. Whatever the reason, late bloomers often find themselves leading lives of tiring and often thankless service to people, institutions, and value systems that have little to do with their own true values or identities. I hope the exercises in chapter 2 helped you to identify a new and more authentic definition of success, one that begins to free you from this system of self-denial. However, I suspect that you may find it hard to put this new definition to work until you become a little more fully centered within yourself.

At first, the essential work of honoring yourself may feel more like an act of betrayal than one of benevolent self-respect. It can be incredibly hard to quit jobs, set new boundaries on old, intrusive relationships, or stand up for what you want in life, especially when it means letting others down. Sometimes your new self-centered actions may feel like embarrassing lapses into self-indulgence. You may find it really hard to explain to your life partner, family, and even your friends why you are going back to school at the age of forty-five, taking a few months off from work to clear your head, or going on a weekend-long retreat to center yourself. Along with a sense of guilt ranging from the vague to the overwhelming, you may experience fear and anxiety as you try to shrug off outgrown modes of being. You may have a very hard time imagining that you can enjoy financial remuneration, social regard, love, and respect for doing what you really want to do.

For all of these reasons, "Honor yourself" is the very first principle of unconventional wisdom. It is the foundation upon which all of the other principles stand. You must strip away the false identities you have forged, let go of the small satisfaction that comes from fulfilling external expectations, and discover the much deeper sense of fulfillment that comes from exposing and exulting in your true identity. There is no question that this process will involve struggle and sacrifice. You must be prepared to sacrifice the false self you have created and to defend with your life the true self that has been waiting in the wings. The story of Marty, a late-blooming artist, provides a vivid example.

Marty had always been a very creative person. Yet the powerful dictates of the traditional southern society in which she grew up, combined with her own low self-esteem, steered her away from expressing her creative talents for many years. In her twenties, she found it easier "to give in to what was expected of a southern woman in the '50s and '60s, and become a housewife and a Junior Leaguer." Marty quit college to marry at the age of twenty-one, started a family, and found few opportunities to express her creative interests until she began to garden. Soon she discovered that she was so good at gardening—and at communicating her knowledge and enthusiasm about it to others—that she was featured in seminars, on local television, and in the newspaper. Marty began to find new self-esteem as others recognized her talents. And in her spare time, she began painting small watercolors, although she rarely showed them to anyone.

After several years of being what she called "a closet painter," Marty attended a course in time management offered by the Junior League. This course provided her with the tools and awareness she needed to begin honoring her talents in a much more ambitious and focused way. "Three days into the course, I realized that I was learning the basic skills I needed to pursue the work I had always longed to do. At the age of thirty-three, I realized that I was an artist, and that I didn't have time for anything else, except my children." Soon after this revelation, Marty began taking every art course she could. She started painting, exhibiting her paintings in group shows, and even winning awards. She was elated by her new pursuits, but her family was frightened by her passion.

"They thought I had gone crazy—that I belonged in an institution," she laughs. "There was a whole ripple effect among my family members, who were used to thinking of me in a different light. It took me years to understand their reactions, and to realize that I had to defend my choices with my new life," she added.

At the same time, Marty's marriage began to disintegrate, and it ultimately ended in divorce. She attended family therapy sessions, and in one of these the therapist asked, "Who is the most important person in your life?" Marty replied, "I'm embarrassed to say this, but the answer is me." Her therapist congratulated her for her answer, exclaiming, "You win the prize! You are going to recover early from this. Love and respect yourself! From now on, it's going to be your life."

While she recovered from her divorce, Marty dedicated herself with even more energy to her painting and began to find creative ways to succeed as an artist. She rented a gallery to show her paintings, against the advice of family members who thought the risk of failure was too great. "I had to prove that I could succeed not only to myself, but also to all the doubters," Marty recalls. And proof came on the opening night of her show, when she sold enough paintings to cover the first year's rent. Marty has been painting and selling her artwork ever since. Today, her gallery is popular with both local and out-of-town art collectors, her artwork is featured in one-woman shows across the country, and she has been the subject of numerous national magazine articles and television shows.

Well aware of the many roadblocks encountered by people when they start to follow their hearts, Marty is generous in her advice. "Find out who you are and what your talents and passions are," she advises late bloomers, "even though our society doesn't always encourage you to do this. If you have trouble, go to a professional who can help you identify your real interests. Put a value on yourself and your work. Do what you love to do . . . and damn the torpedoes!"

As Marty's story demonstrates, when late bloomers begin to discern and follow their true callings, there will be times when they will have to temporarily forfeit the approval of others and persevere in the face of criticism and doubt. These times challenge late bloomers deeply. "Making such basic changes in your life must lead to changes in your relationships, and this can be very unnerving," Marty recalls.

But Marty's example demonstrates that if you can arm yourself ahead of time by finding that place inside yourself where you know who you are and what you value, you will find it much easier to weather these storms. "I learned to enjoy risk once I realized how big the loss of never risking at all could be," Marty explains. Once you begin to honor yourself, you will begin to exult in your new life even as the old one tags along and tugs at your newfound self-esteem. Like Marty, you will discover that the joy of creatively expressing yourself is worth far more than the empty rewards you once struggled so hard to earn.

EXERCISES

Meditation: Remembering bliss

I encourage you to begin honoring yourself now by remembering what you truly love and admire about yourself. Use this meditation to reconnect with the healthy, pleasant self-centeredness most of us experienced in childhood, when the self, with all its likes and dislikes, passions and quirks, was freely expressed in play, especially during solitary play. Such play connected you not only with yourself, but also with the world around you, engaging you in a celebration of its many gifts. If you can't remember connecting with yourself in this way, then pick any memory that helps to reconnect you with a sense of pleasurable self-centeredness.

1. Sit in a comfortable place where you are unlikely to be disturbed by the telephone or other interruptions. Close your eyes and breathe naturally, focusing on your breath, until the racing thoughts about all the things you should, or could, be doing begin to slow down and fade away.

2. After a relaxed minute or two, remember what it was like when you were a child playing by yourself. What were some of your favorite things to do? Pick one of these activities and focus upon it. Fully flesh out your memory of it. Where were you? What were your surroundings like? What was so satisfying about the activity you pursued? Remember the details of the activity, and reexperience each part as completely as you can.

3. What innate interests, talents, and passions did you express and even celebrate in this activity? In what way did the activity connect you with yourself? In what way

did it connect you with the gifts of the world around you? Remember what it felt like to do something purely for the pleasure of it, not because doing so pleased others.

4. Now, return your attention to your present life. Is there any activity that you engage in today which uses these same interests, talents, and passions, or gives you the same sense of pleasure and satisfaction? What, if anything, gets in the way of your pure enjoyment or surrender to this activity?

5. Imagine you are engaged in this activity right now, and you've brought to it that pure and lively sense of pleasure that you experienced as a child. Can you imagine a way of making this activity even more pleasurable and satisfying? What can you do differently to help overcome the resistance that interferes with your pleasure and focus?

6. End your meditation with a promise to yourself to pursue the activity you just imagined, in this new way, in the very near future.

Exercise: Know thyself

If you look closely enough, you will probably find that your personality traits—your unique characteristics, passions, interests, and tendencies—fall into two overlapping categories: aspects you value, and aspects others value. We tend to place too much emphasis on developing the aspects that others value because we are rewarded from an early age for doing so. As a result, we often neglect aspects of ourselves that we actually value much more highly. Without even realizing it, we may be invalidating, and even betraying, some of our most essential and delightful gifts. This not-so-benign neglect typically leads to frustration, disappointing levels of satisfaction and fulfillment in life, and feelings of emptiness and worthlessness. This writing exercise will help you gain greater clarity about these two different personality subsets.

To set the proper tone for this exercise, you must carefully choose where you are going to complete it. Find a place where you can be truly comfortable—a place that both nurtures and pleases you. This might be a chair on the beach, or a spot underneath a tree in a nearby park. It might be in your own bedroom or garden, or in a church on a pew, or on a bench in an art museum. Make sure it is a place where you feel removed from the everyday demands of your life and where you won't be interrupted. Go there with your notepad and pencil and begin the exercise, using the format from the worksheet provided.

Before answering the questions, take a few minutes to breathe deeply, clear your mind, and get comfortable and relaxed. Then read each question carefully and begin writing your answers. Try to let your responses travel directly from your brain to the paper, without too much thinking, analyzing, or editing. Stop only when you are sure you have nothing else to add. Take a look at the example provided if you need a little extra help getting started.

1. What aspects of yourself—your own particular character-istics, passions, interests, or tendencies—do you most cherish, admire, value, and respect? Try to stay honest as you make this list. Be sure that the aspects you describe are ones that you value from a place deep within yourself, not because you have been told by others that they are lik-able, admirable, valuable, and respectable qualities. Your list may include aspects that have lain dormant for a long time but which you've longed to revive.

2. When you are done, read back over this list and place dashes next to those aspects you do express in your daily

life, through your work, play, leisure, home, or family life, or in your surroundings, spiritual practices, and so on.

3. Read the list again and place stars next to those aspects you tend to repress or ignore for long periods of time.

4. Now make a list of those aspects you have been taught to value or have cultivated because they are valued, condoned, and rewarded by the outside world. These may be *characteristics* (a tendency to place others' concerns before your own), *attributes* (being organized), or *skills* (the ability to design software). You might find that some of these overlap with items on your list of aspects that you value about yourself. That is fine; put them down anyway.

5. When you are done, read this second list and ask yourself, honestly, whether these are aspects you still want to express in your daily life. Do they describe the person whom you know yourself to be, deep inside, or whom you wish to become? Will they help you to achieve the vision you have described for yourself? If so, note how you can turn these traits to your advantage. If not, cross them off your list . . . and pay attention to how you feel as you do this—gleeful, guilty, or just plain relieved.

EXAMPLE

Exercise: Know thyself

List aspects of yourself that you truly, deeply value:

* my love of beauty
* my ability to paint and draw
- my drive and energy
* my enthusiasm for life
* my loving nature
* my ability to marvel at the world and be inspired by it
* my sense of the absurd
* my desire to break the rules and live on my own terms
- my sense of humor

Place stars next to the items above that you tend to repress in your daily life; put dashes next to the ones that you express on a regular basis.

List aspects of yourself that others value and reward:

my ability to sell things (this will help me sell my artwork)
my willingness to work very hard to fulfill others' expectations
my desire to please others (this, along with the desire to please myself, will help me create quality artwork)
my fear of failure
my ability to be organized (I can use this to be more effective in my new career)
my willingness to put myself last at work and in relationships
my energy and enthusiasm (this will fuel me in my career change)

Cross off the items above that do *not* describe the person you want to be or will *not* help you achieve your new vision; note how the items you don't cross off may help you to achieve your vision.

Exercise: Know thyself

List aspects of yourself that you truly, deeply value:

_____

_____

_____

_____

_____

_____

_____

_____

_____

Place stars next to the items above that you tend to repress in your daily life; put dashes next to the ones that you express on a regular basis.

List aspects of yourself that others value and reward:

_____

_____

_____

_____

_____

_____

_____

_____

_____

Cross off the items above that do *not* describe the person you want to be or will *not* help you achieve your new vision; note how the items you don't cross off may help you to achieve your vision.

Pursuit: To thine own self be true

Are you ready to express those aspects of yourself that you have been ignoring or repressing for a long time? Are you ready for a delightful, delicious day of honoring yourself? If you act upon your conviction that you value a certain aspect of yourself, you will probably discover how truly valuable that aspect is to you and to the world. And you may well find that you are much less likely to ignore this part of yourself in the future.

One night, before you go to bed, reread the list you made of the aspects you most admire in yourself. Pay particularly close attention to those you placed stars by—the ones you tend to neglect in your daily life. Leave the list near your bed, and when you wake up in the morning, read it again. Make a promise to yourself to be as aware as you can of these aspects throughout the day, and to try, whenever possible, to express them in your actions and attitudes. Any time you feel the desire to do something during the day that honors these aspects, do it! Be conscious throughout the day of how differently you feel about yourself and the world.

My guess is that you will find this experience so exhilarating that you will want to repeat it again and again. That's the point! Great rewards come from honoring yourself. The more honest you are about your true values and interests, and the more devotedly you pursue and express them, the sooner you can begin to lead an authentic, rewarding, and deeply satisfying life. If you can, begin practicing this pursuit on a regular basis. You will find greater success and happiness immediately.

CHAPTER 5

Second Principle of Unconventional Wisdom

Believe and You Will See

How many times has someone said to you, "I'll believe it when I see it"? This is the kind of person who insisted that the world was flat, that people would never fly, and that man would never walk upon the moon. If we all abided by this limiting credo, we wouldn't have pyramids, cathedrals, or skyscrapers. We wouldn't have printed books, electric lights, CD players, or computers. Much of the architecture, science, and technology that we take for granted today exists because visionaries imagined something, then worked hard to translate their inner visions into external reality. These people believed in their visions while others scoffed at them and considered them weird. And, as a result, we now live in a universe that is enriched by the fruit of their faith and hard work. These creative and determined souls provide an alternative credo by which late bloomers can live: "Believe and you will see."

By now, I hope that you have succeeded in describing the life you want to live. If you want that life to become a reality, you must begin to live as if you actually believe that it will come to pass. If you are serious about making a life change, it will no longer be possible for you to go on saying, "I wish I could be a ____." You must start declaring, at least to yourself: "I will become a ____," or, even better, "I am a ____." Then you can begin taking actions that will be fueled by that belief. For example, I went around for years thinking, and occasionally saying out loud, "I wish I could become a writer." But until I actually believed that this was possible and began taking action by writing proposals and mailing them to editors, this wish had little or no chance of becoming a reality.

I know from experience that this is much more easily said than done. Just as it is difficult to begin honoring yourself, it is also difficult to believe in your dream. These stumbling blocks can trip late bloomers up for years. Sometimes this happens because people repeatedly tell you that your dream is impossible. (I can't tell you how many times I have been told that it is impossible to make a living as a writer. I love proving these naysayers wrong.) Maybe you haven't seen any evidence that others have succeeded in the area that most appeals to you, or you haven't found any role models yet to show you the way. Perhaps certain relationships or situations have eroded both your sense of self-esteem and your faith in the generosity of the universe to support your dreams.

Unfortunately, you may have received many messages from the outside world that undercut what you know to be true about your gifts and their potential for fruitful expression. But you can invite new energy into your life, and you can seek out the new people and new experiences that will reinforce your faith in yourself and your vision. The story of John, another late-blooming artist, demonstrates the transforming power of faith, supported by action, to make our dreams come true.

"I always loved everything visual," John recalls. When he was a child, he was drawn to the beauty of fishermen and sailing vessels, displays in a local museum, art books, even to the advertisements on the sides of vegetable crates. Although he showed an early aptitude for drawing, John performed poorly in every other subject at school because of a severe, undiagnosed case of dyslexia. "I was constantly humiliated in school by having to read out loud," he remembers. "I was held back a grade and graduated second from the bottom of my class. No one had any expectations for me, and I had horribly low self-esteem."

John was discouraged from entering the arts as a profession by his family, who did not consider it a satisfactory way to make a living. At the age of twenty, demoralized by their discouragement, his painful experiences in school, and early symptoms of what was to become full-blown alcoholism, he gave up his dream of being a painter. He joined the Coast Guard, then attended college on the GI Bill, graduating with a degree in journalism after six grueling years of studies still complicated by his dyslexia.

Even though John had given up on being an artist, others kept recognizing his talent and offering him opportunities. Perhaps that was because he chose to surround himself with creative people. At college, where he studied graphic arts, John met a classmate who saw how well he drew. This friend recruited John to be a graphic artist for an advertising agency upon his graduation. After John worked for a few years in this field, another friend recognized his potential as a fine artist and gave him $1000 to help him launch his career as a painter. "He saw a talent I didn't see," John says. "He thought I should be an artist."

By accepting his friend's gift and devoting his days to painting, John began to reconnect with his childhood passion. "I was thirty years old, and I had no idea how much I had been repressing," he confesses. "A tremendous amount of energy was released and I painted like a maniac." But by the time John reconnected with his calling as a painter, his faith in himself and the world was so eroded by low self-esteem and alcoholism that he could barely function. For several years he continued to paint, selling a few paintings while making ends meet with odd jobs, but he couldn't focus his full energies on his art career. "I was drinking more and more," he remembers. "I had panic attacks, agoraphobia, tremendous hangovers. I had such low self-esteem, I didn't believe that I could really succeed at anything."

John reached yet another turning point nine years later. "I finally went to a 12-step program for help when I was thirty-nine," he explains, "and I count that as when I began my life as a late bloomer." As part of his recovery from alcoholism, John experienced a spiritual awakening. "I tried to take the train to sobriety, and ended up on the train to spirituality," he recalls, and it was this experience that finally helped him to believe in, and actively pursue, his vision of being a successful artist. "I began to believe that I belonged in this world, that I had something of value to contribute," he recalls, and this new attitude began to show up in the work that he did. "My post-sobriety art is filled with light—the light of love, as well as the light of the sun," he explains.

As John began to have more faith in himself, he also discovered a new quality in his business skills. He began to actively seek lucrative commissions from a range of corporate clients to pay the bills while he established himself as a fine artist. Once he began selling his fine art to a growing number of private patrons, he opened his own gallery, which became one of the most financially successful galleries in his hometown. He even wrote an autobiography describing his experiences and struggles, which quickly sold out its first printing.

What late bloomers can learn from John's experience is the importance of supporting your vision with your faith. Even though John reconnected with his artistic calling by the time he was thirty, he did not become a successful, self-supporting artist until he actually began to believe that this calling had the power to flourish, and began acting on that faith. He had to contradict the external messages he had received from his family and community as well as his own internal messages of worthlessness and hopelessness. When he did so, he was able not only to paint with more energy and authenticity, but also to market his work and sell it more effectively. Once he began to act as if he believed he could be a financially successful artist, he laid the necessary groundwork to become one.

Certainly, John was fortunate in finding friends and a recovery program that provided him with a support network for this process. But all late bloomers can get the help they need. A wide range of self-help and counseling programs are easily accessible to those who need help in discerning their aptitudes and translating them into careers. Just look up the subject of career counseling on the Internet, in your local yellow pages, or at the library or bookstore. There are also trade associations for just about every craft and profession that exists. Through the associations, you can meet other people who share your interests and can learn more about how to get started or get ahead. Late bloomers can find guidance and support through individual therapy and counseling, non-religious support groups, 12-step programs, continuing education centers, churches, synagogues, and many other such sources.

As you grow clearer about the vision you want to pursue, you will become more conscious of the people around you who are engaged in similar pursuits. Seek these people out and spend time with them—they can become the friends and mentors who will speed you along your path. Individuals have long sought out communities of like-minded peers, whether in utopian societies, monasteries and convents, artist colonies, or other kinds of intentional communities. You can create your own intentional community by populating your life with people who live in the realm of possibility, who believe in you, and who will help you to believe in yourself and your dream.

In addition to searching the outside world for individuals who can serve as examples, inspirations, and supporters, you will also need to look within. Again, you need to learn how to consider your vision for the future a reality, not just a fantasy. By dreaming about your future in vivid color, you can actually bring it closer. I encourage you to daydream about the life you want to live as often as possible, and to find ways to translate these dreams into reality on a regular basis. As soon as you begin putting the power of your faith *and* your actions behind your dream, I guarantee that your life will begin to change. Are you ready to begin?

EXERCISES

Meditation: This perfect moment

In the exercises in chapter 3, you described your vision for the future. In this exercise, I invite you to mentally travel into that future and imagine yourself living there. This exercise can be practiced any time you have fifteen minutes to shut your eyes and allow your mind to wander. (I often practice it on the stationary bike at the gym or while soaking in the bathtub.)

1. Reread or recall the vision statement you wrote and imagine living the full life that vision describes: Imagine how great you feel when you wake up in the morning, what exciting activities you do during the day, and where you go and how you feel as you pursue your passion. Imagine moments of leisure and work, and the rhythm of your full life in all its variety. Feel how very natural it seems, how almost inevitable this future is—if you simply allow yourself to believe in who you are and what you want.

2. When you feel that you have allowed your vision of the future to play out in all its glorious detail, try to select a single image of yourself living that new life that "says it all." Select a moment that reveals you completely engaged in the calling you have discerned—a moment in which you experience the rewards of the life you want to lead. If you want to be an actor, perhaps this moment is captured in a vision of you on the stage, delivering a dramatic monologue. If you want to carve out more time for leisure activities like hiking, then perhaps you are alone in the wilderness.

3. Focus your inner vision a little longer on that perfect moment and allow your imagination to furnish it with as many details as you can. Imagine that you are composing a painting, a photograph, a movie scene, or a stage set. What exactly are you wearing? What are your surroundings like—the sights, the sounds, the smells? What time of day is it? Who else is there? Keep arranging the details until you have composed an image that fully expresses the beauty, significance, and desirability of this perfect moment.

4. Now, think about how you can translate this moment into reality—sooner rather than later. You may not actually be

able to put all the details into place, but surely you can re-create aspects of this perfect moment in real life before long. For example, the would-be actor could perform a monologue for a group of friends, or perhaps even audition for a community theater production. The would-be hiker may not be able to fly out to the Rockies for the perfect wilderness experience, but there must be a nature trail nearby that can offer an hour's pleasure. What do you need to do to re-create this moment in your real life? How can you arrange these details? When can you do it? Make it soon.

5. Now, open your eyes and look at the world around you. It probably looks different: slightly less hard and limiting, and slightly more expansive and full of potential. You probably feel different, too, having experienced a fleshed-out vision of your future, not as a pipe dream that will soon disappear into a puff of smoke but as a tangible, accessible reality.

Pursuit: Making dreams come true

In order to translate your dreams into reality, you need to prove that you believe in them by taking concrete actions. You can begin practicing this now by translating the perfect moment you just envisioned into a real-time, real-place experience. Circle a date in your calendar to experience your perfect moment. Then, make a list of any resources you will need and actions you will have to take to create this perfect moment (see the worksheet and example provided). Start completing the items on your checklist so you will be ready by the date you have set. When the time arrives, don't get hung up if you can't get everything you need; make do with what you have gotten. After all, life is rarely perfect.

When the date arrives, make your dream come true and enjoy it. Spend as much time living your dream as you can and savor the experience. Fully engage in the activities you want to pursue. Allow yourself to experience the rewards. Focus on everything that goes right and don't allow yourself to get negative if some little thing goes wrong. While the moment in your meditation was perfect, you can't expect it to be quite so flawless in real life. Just enjoy the moment you have created for yourself and continue to believe in and be inspired by your vision. If you do, you will discover the faith and the energy you need to translate your perfect moment into reality on a regular basis.

EXAMPLE

Pursuit: Making dreams come true

Describe your perfect moment:

I am at the opening of an exhibition of my own paintings. It is in a beautiful, sophisticated art gallery with high ceilings and natural wood floors. There is a trio playing jazz in the corner; champagne is flowing. I am standing by one of my paintings, discussing it with an avid collector of my work. I am wearing a great red dress. My dealer is across the room selling paintings. My friends are everywhere. They are amazed at how my work has progressed. People I don't even know are admiring and purchasing my paintings!

Describe how you can translate this dream into a real experience soon:

I could finish the painting I started last week and make two more paintings over the next three weeks, then have a little cocktail party and invite my friends to see my new work. I could have jazz music playing on the stereo, wear a fabulous red dress, even make up a price list for the paintings, just in case anyone wants to buy one. I could ask my friend Ellen to act as my "dealer," answering questions friends have about my work and, if needed, actually taking care of any sales that occur. I'll offer her a commission so that she really is acting as my dealer.

Set a date when you can act out your dream: November 11

List the resources you will need and actions you must take, and check them off as you work through your list:

Check	Resources/Actions
_____	Make the paintings
_____	Talk to Ellen about being my dealer for the evening
_____	Create a guest list, design an invitation, and mail it
_____	Plan food, beverages, music, and flowers for the party
_____	Type up a price list
_____	Hang the paintings
_____	Put on my red dress and GO!

Now, make your dream come true!

WORKSHEET

Pursuit: Making dreams come true

Describe your perfect moment:

_____

_____

_____

_____

_____

_____

_____

_____

Describe how you can translate this dream into a real experience soon:

_____

_____

_____

_____

_____

_____

_____

_____

Set a date when you can act out your dream:
List the resources you will need and actions you must take, and check them off as you work through your list:

Check   Resources/Actions

_____   _____

_____   _____

_____   _____

_____   _____

_____   _____

_____   _____

_____   _____

Now, make your dream come true!

CHAPTER 6

Third Principle of Unconventional Wisdom

Leap Before You Look

When I was a child, I had a dream about heaven. In the dream, a host of animals led me to the brink of a cliff beyond which a stony chasm yawned. One by one, the animals leapt off the cliff into the thin air and sprouted wings, but only *after* they had leapt. Naturally skeptical in such extraordinary circumstances, I held back until there was only a single beast left on the edge of the earth with me. When I asked the animal what was on the other side of the chasm, he informed me that it was heaven and that the only way to get there was by jumping off the cliff. I demanded of him, "But how do I know that I will grow wings?" Leaping into the brink, he answered me: "You won't, until you jump."

Conventional wisdom warns us not to leap before we look. From a practical standpoint, this makes a world of sense. How can we gauge the amount of energy we'll need or estimate the length of the jump we'll have to make unless we take a good, hard look? But anyone who has stood too long gazing into the breach, measuring its breadth, imagining its depth, pondering the consequences of falling short, and, ultimately, questioning the desirability of the destination, knows how quickly looking can lead to utter paralysis. While it is a good idea to glance ahead, staring into the gap can be just as treacherous as jumping off blindfolded.

When it comes to pursuing life dreams, there are plenty of famous achievers who followed their hearts by hurtling heedlessly into the unknown, seemingly unconcerned about the potential consequences to their health, pocketbooks, family members, and friends. They simply leapt, and often enough, they grew wings. Wolfgang Amadeus Mozart comes to mind as one renowned example. The music which he began to produce at the precocious age of five is nothing short of heavenly. But the mercurial rises and falls in fortune that accompanied his brief and brilliant career would terrify the average late bloomer. Veering from court favorite to impoverished invalid, Mozart's life seems to be one that few of us would desire to lead, yet who among us doesn't wish that we possessed a tiny measure of his genius and his pure devotion to his gift?

Imagine, for a moment, that Mozart was not a precocious prodigy after all, but rather a late bloomer. What might have happened if his father had said, "Wolfie, look before you leap!" and Mozart had done so? What if he had agreed that his prospects for financial security as a composer were too slim, and instead accepted the position of assistant court stenographer? "Take a letter, Mozart," his master might have said. And Mozart would have listened through clouds of music to some dry treatise, scribbling it down with a heavy heart. Before long, Mozart would probably have died of boredom or misery, or he might have gotten fired. Or, worst yet, he might have lived a long and empty life, void of the pure joy and beauty that clearly transported him above the adversity he faced during his capricious existence, and to this day gives tremendous pleasure to millions of people.

Several of the problems with looking too long before you leap are illustrated by this absurd rewriting of history. Leaping is an act of courage inspired by a combination of *desire* to achieve a certain outcome, *conviction* (if only a temporary one) in your powers and gifts, *devotion* (and even submission) to your calling, and a burst of *faith* that the universe will somehow honor and sustain that path. Looking is a rational act that is, by its very nature, at odds with the more or less irrational qualities of desire, conviction, devotion, and faith.

In other words, if you want to follow your heart, the best way to do so probably isn't to send your rational mind out to survey the road. More than likely, it will come back and tell your heart that the road is impassable. On the other hand, if you only send your most irrational and passionate aspects out to chart a path, the course they recommend might prove overly ambitious and impractical. Nonetheless, a wholehearted attempt at an impractical course has more chance of success than a halfhearted surrender to the status quo.

The advice of your rational mind, as well as that of concerned family or friends, is based all too often on values that have no relevance to the desires that burn in your soul. For example, a person with a stable job, a modest salary, and benefits might be told by a concerned friend that it would be foolish to give these things up for the uncertainty of a new career as, say, a caterer. "After all," this friend might argue, "there are already so many caterers out there. And what would you do if the demand for caterers dried up? There you would be, without a steady salary, without benefits, with nothing but quail egg on your face."

What this prognosis fails to take into consideration is, in short, everything that matters to someone who wants to change his or her life. If the modest salary and benefits were sufficient reward, the person receiving them would not be considering an alternate career. In many cases, no amount of salary, benefits, or so-called security is adequate payment for a person who knows that he or she is betraying an urgent calling or a hidden talent. The story of Nikki, a late-blooming magazine publisher, provides a perfect example.

Although Nikki wanted to be a writer when she was a little girl, she took a long detour at the age of seventeen, eloping with her high-school sweetheart, traveling cross-country as a Navy wife, and giving birth to four children in six years. Her first career, as full-time wife and mother, ended abruptly when she and her husband separated and she found herself starting over at the age of twenty-seven as a single mother with no work experience and no advanced education. Fortunately surrounded by a support network of other single mothers and a recipient of government grants, Nikki went to college and graduated with honors. Degree in literature in hand, Nikki soon got her first job as a secretary for a publishing company. Within five years, at the age of forty, Nikki was at the top of her field, promoted to vice-president in charge of a line of computer books and education software.

By many people's standards, Nikki was already in full bloom. But deep down inside, she suspected that she was only beginning to flower. Suffering from a combination of burnout with the corporate publishing environment and empty-nest syndrome (all but one of her children had left home), Nikki decided it was time for another change. Sure that she wasn't satisfied with her current life, but not yet clear about what the next stage would bring, Nikki quit her job and followed a couple of friends to settle in a quiet sea island community. In other words, Nikki leapt before she looked, giving up the safety and security of a job she no longer wanted for a fresh start.

In the beginning, Nikki took odd jobs ranging from house-cleaning to working at a local inn. She began getting freelance writing assignments after a year or two. Having cleared her decks and refocused her creative energies, Nikki was primed for a new vision, and one day it came. She decided that she wanted to publish a magazine for women in her community—an idea that seemed to come out of nowhere and yet be the culmination of an entire lifetime of experience and education.

Within a year of this revelation, Nikki began publishing a magazine called *Skirt!* out of her home office, with the help of a friend who is a graphic designer and a small start-up loan from another friend. Within five years, *Skirt!* reached a monthly circulation of 20,000, and had an estimated readership of 50,000, plus an award-winning web site serving international audiences. Nikki herself writes a monthly column while also editing the work of a stable of freelancers who contribute articles about concerns and interests shared by women.

In an issue of *Skirt!*, Nikki published some advice which clearly spoke from one late bloomer to another: "Get up and get going. Stop waiting and start creating a life story right here right now. Fill it with strange cities and happy homecomings . . . blood, SEX and tears . . . loyal friends . . . worthy adversaries . . . warriors and wise women . . . temptations and failures . . . TRIUMPHS and celebrations . . . solitary journeys . . . visionary gleams . . . love, death and transformation. It's your story . . . make it a page-turner."

When late bloomers decide to change their lives, they have

to be willing to leave the beaten path of the familiar, and bush-whack into the unknown territory of heretofore-denied curiosities, desires, and interests. While some late bloomers may be very clear about what they want to change and ready to move right into that new life, there are many more like Nikki who only know that they are ready for something new. Sometimes late bloomers find they no longer have any choice but to go ahead. They lose their jobs, find themselves suddenly single after years of marriage, or wake up one day and find that their children have left home. In other cases, they voluntarily clear their own decks, quit jobs they hate, end abusive relationships, or buy some free time with extra childcare or other kinds of assistance.

These late bloomers do not always rush right out and get another demanding job or enter into another long-term relationship. Participants in 12-step programs, putting their lives back together as they recover from addictions, often get what they call "recovery jobs" at first—low-stress, low-commitment assignments that allow them to clear their heads and heal their hearts. They also try to avoid new emotional entanglements for one year, while they get clearer about who they really are and what they want from life. Like Nikki, many late bloomers follow this course, taking several months or a year to reorient themselves, replenish their inner resources, and redirect their desires. During this time their perception clears, they learn to listen to their own demands instead of others', and they experiment with new interests or ways of expressing themselves in work, leisure, and relationships.

Even late bloomers who don't feel the need to take time out will still have to prepare to leap at a certain point, even though they won't know what the final destination will be, or feel completely convinced that they will arrive at it safely. When it comes to the business of living our lives, so many late bloomers stifle the very instincts that might lead them to greater fulfillment and success, and decide against investing time or money in adventures that are informed by hunches or pure curiosity. We find ourselves wondering what our friends, spouses, or family members might say. We conjure up images of people we know who took off on tangents and never came back, remaining in patchouli-scented worlds of outmoded hippy detachment. We're afraid that will happen to us if we take up this hobby, sign up for this course, or take on that volunteer commitment.

I invite you to consider the alternative—to imagine that by pursuing the urgings of your hidden desires, you will experience nothing but the most affirming and rewarding success. Just remember—your heart may fly to your throat, your pulse may race, and your feet might even slip as you scramble for one last foothold on familiar ground. But ultimately, by calling upon your inner resources of desire, conviction, devotion, and faith, you can counteract the resignation, skepticism, resistance, and fear that has kept you glued to the spot for far too long.

Once you have looked not only with your outer eye but also with your inner vision, you must then stop looking and start leaping. Only then will you discover the inner resources of strength and the outward signs of abundance that the world offers to those who dare to trust in it. Are you ready to leap? Your future awaits on the other side.

EXERCISES

Meditation: Practice jumps

In the previous exercises, you allowed yourself to flesh out your vision of the future. In this meditation, you can rehearse the journey that will transport you there, imagining what it will feel like when you jump from the firm ground of the familiar into the unknown. You will imagine both the fear and the exhilaration you will experience as your feet leave the ground and, through doing so, you will be better prepared to take this action in real life.

1. Take a few moments to revisit your vision of the life that you want to lead. Conjure up that perfect moment and allow yourself to experience it once more in your imagination.

2. Now, step back into the present and contrast the life you have just imagined with the one you lead today. How is your present life different? What are the activities that take up your time, and what feelings fill your waking and sleeping hours? Bring forth that person within you who reluctantly shows up every day to do the work that must be done, yet burns with desire to make a change.

3. Now, imagine a moment *in the very near future* when you give that restless being inside you the permission to bridge the gap between your current life and the future you desire so strongly. Imagine each major action that you will take to translate your vision into reality. At what point must you loosen your grasp upon the known, familiar life and leap into the unknown? What step seems truly difficult—or even impossible—for you to take? When does that Chorus of No begin to shout, "No! No! No! You are about to make *A Big Mistake!*"?

4. Stop there for a moment. Instead of listening any longer to those voices and staring, paralyzed, into the chasm that yawns between you and this next step, leap. Simply leap. Imagine how far toward your destination you can advance. Certainly, there are risks. But focus instead upon the rewards. Imagine cutting loose, whether this means risk-

ing your reputation, your current job, or your financial stability, and try to allow yourself to experience the elation that can come when you throw caution to the wind and follow your heart. Imagine the jolt of energy you will experience when you take this step.

5. Finally, allow yourself to imagine arriving safely on the other side. How could the courage that you mustered to take this leap unleash a torrent of success? Allow your imagination to run wild as you envision the ease with which your dream can come true when you pursue it armed with self-respect, faith, and courage.

Pursuit: Leaping into action

Are you prepared to stop looking and start leaping in real life? You may be ready to apply this pursuit to a task directly related to the life change you want to make. Or you may want to practice at first with something less stressful. However you use it, this pursuit can be practiced again and again until the benefits derived from it become second nature. The example and worksheet provided will help to guide you through this process.

1. Select an activity that you have always had a touch of curiosity about or felt a gravitational pull toward. This might be related to your hidden desire, like taking a paralegal course if you are interested in becoming a lawyer, or catering a party if professional cooking is a stifled interest. Or it might be completely unrelated, like taking a dance class or going sea kayaking. Just pick something about which you have mingled feelings of attraction and resistance or anxiety.

2. Make a short list of all the pleasant results, both tangible and intangible, that might follow from pursuing this activity. Notice how the Chorus of No keeps trying to put in its two cents, pointing out all the reasons why you can't or shouldn't pursue this activity. Make a list of these as well. Leave the list of pleasant results out in a highly visible location. Put the list of "Noes" away in a drawer.

3. Make a list of the steps required to complete this activity, whether requesting a catalogue from a local continuing education program, looking something up in the yellow pages, searching the Internet, or calling a friend who can help. Take these actions within the day (or, if that's truly impossible, within the week).

4. As soon as possible, actively begin the pursuit itself. Pay attention to the pleasure you experience along the way. And if you falter, or start to become anxious, remember that this pursuit isn't about doing things perfectly. It is about exploring and discovering new potential. We could never have learned to walk without falling, and we had to babble nonsense for years before we learned to speak sense.

5. When you have completed the pursuit, take the time to congratulate yourself for trying something you didn't think you could achieve.

Through practicing this pursuit again and again, you will find that you have some experience under your belt when you arrive at the point of no return and have to take a great leap toward your future.

EXAMPLE

Pursuit: Leaping into action

Select an activity that you have always had a touch of curiosity about or felt a gravitational pull toward, whether it is directly related to the vision you want to follow or is completely unrelated, and use the following steps to leap into action.

1. Describe the activity you have in mind and explain why it is calling out to you:

   Taking a belly dancing class—I want to try a new dance form that will allow me to express my sensuality and break free from my inhibitions.

2. Make a short list of all the pleasant results that might follow from pursuing this activity, both tangible and intangible:

   I might find a new hobby—a pleasurable form of exercise; I might reconnect with my childhood love of dancing and tap into new sources of creative energy that would flow into other parts of my life. I might let go of some inhibitions.

3. Write another list of any negative results that you think might occur, however irrational they may seem:

   I might look and feel like an idiot and set off a whole attack of low self-esteem. Instead of releasing inhibitions, I might reinforce them. What if I pull a muscle?

4. List the steps you must take in order to finish this activity and check them off as you complete them:

   ✓ Call the dance studio and find out class schedule
   ✓ Figure out what I'm going to wear
   ✓ Schedule class in my calendar
   ✓ Go to class

5. Leap into action, and when you are done, write a few words describing your experience: what benefits you gained, what fears failed to materialize, what, if anything, went wrong, and how you dealt with it. End with a few words of praise for yourself—for your courage, sense of adventure, and willingness to grow.

I ended up loving the class. The movements were difficult and I did look like an idiot, but I didn't care because it was a beginners' class and everyone else looked pretty silly, too. We laughed a lot. The music was great and at the end, I felt energized and alive. The experience made me realize that I don't have to do everything perfectly. I am proud of myself for being willing to try something new and risk looking foolish!

WORKSHEET

Pursuit: Leaping into action

Select an activity that you have always had a touch of curiosity about or felt a gravitational pull toward, whether it is directly related to the vision you want to follow or is completely unrelated, and use the following steps to leap into action.

1. Describe the activity you have in mind and explain why it is calling out to you:

_____
_____
_____
_____

2. Make a short list of all the pleasant results that might follow from pursuing this activity, both tangible and intangible:

_____
_____
_____
_____

3. Write another list of any negative results that you think might occur, however irrational they may seem:

_____
_____
_____
_____

4. List the steps you must take in order to finish this activity and check them off as you complete them:

___ _____
___ _____
___ _____
___ _____

5. Leap into action, and when you are done, write a few words describing your experience: what benefits you gained, what fears failed to materialize, what, if anything, went wrong, and how you dealt with it. End with a few words of praise for yourself—for your courage, sense of adventure, and willingness to grow.

_____

_____

_____

_____

_____

_____

_____

CHAPTER 7

Fourth Principle of Unconventional Wisdom

Bite Off More Than You Can Chew

Swallow your pride. Take a bitter pill. Bite the bullet. Unlike the proverbs we have turned on their heads, these common expressions provide excellent wisdom for late bloomers. The actions which you must take in order to change your life often involve swallowing your pride, if you interpret pride as that false sense of self-worth that is based upon others' high opinions. You may have to forfeit the praise, respect, and position that are associated with the walk of life you have decided to leave behind and be willing to become a beginner again. Often when you "swallow your pride," you discover that you are filled to bursting with self-respect.

At first, taking the steps that will change your life may feel like eating a bitter pill. Admitting that you may need to surprise or disappoint your boss or family members, go back to school, scale back on your spending, or work longer hours in order to launch a new career or follow an insistent calling may feel like downing an unpleasant dose of medicine. But as anyone who has ever had a shot of penicillin or a spoonful of cough syrup knows, relief from suffering and improved well-being are soon to follow, and are well worth the temporary discomfort that treatment requires.

Back in the days before modern anesthesia, the only form of relief available for people undergoing surgery was to bite the bullet—literally. There will be times when you, too, will have to bite the bullet and endure an inevitable amount of pain as you perform surgery upon your life. Yet I can promise you that the lifesaving effects of this surgery will ultimately offset the temporary suffering you may experience.

Unfortunately, each one of these sayings invokes the concept of pain or discomfort—things that we all naturally shy away from. So I would like to suggest a more appetizing morsel of oral wisdom to help you on your way: Bite off more than you can chew!

When it comes to eating, many of us bite off more than we can chew from time to time, especially when no one is looking. We surrender to our desire to devour a particularly tantalizing dish and end up with more food in our mouths than we can politely chew. Our cheeks bulge and our eyes water. Perhaps we even have to chew with our mouths open for a minute or two. Then we swallow and savor the moment of greedy pleasure we have allowed ourselves. The price we must pay for our moment of gleeful indulgence may be a moment of mild discomfort and embarrassment as we grapple with the object of our desire, but, all in all, this is a story with a happy ending. Man bites hot dog—whole.

The polite alternative, "Don't bite off more than you can chew," is actually one of the worst pieces of advice I have ever encountered, and one that late bloomers should start to ignore *right now.* The only way to get ahead in this life is by biting off more than you can chew, again and again and again. If you honestly scrutinize your life, you will see that you have bitten off more than you could chew many times.

How often have you agreed to do something, only to realize a moment later that you don't have the slightest idea how you are going to do it? Perhaps your boss asks you to do something you've never done before. "Do you think you can handle that?" she might inquire. "Of course," you reply, outwardly wanting to please and impress while inwardly wondering how on earth you are going to pull it off. Perhaps a friend calls up and asks you to lend a hand with a volunteer commitment. More than likely, you say "Yes," before you have even figured out how you are going to find the time. Or maybe you decide to bake a cake from scratch to celebrate a beloved's birthday. Once you have assembled all the ingredients and given the instructions a careful reading, you realize that this will be much harder than you thought at first. But by then you've already promised, and you don't want to let your loved one down.

Why is it, then, that you have so much trouble biting off more than you can chew when it comes to fulfilling your own desires? Instead of taking a big bite, do you just stare with a watering mouth at the tempting meal that is your future? The stories of late bloomers whom I have interviewed, as well as my own personal experience, point toward two powerful forces that explain why you may have found it easier to tackle tough challenges in your old life than in pursuit of the new life you want to lead.

One of these forces is the power of *momentum.* Momentum is rarely on your side when you enact life change. Usually your past experience slows you down, or hurtles you along an entirely different path, up steep hills and over rushing streams that you were not even interested in crossing. You scale the heights and jump over the depths—not because you want to, or even because you think you can, but simply because the momentum of your life drives you forward. Perhaps your past success in the work you find yourself doing bolsters your confidence. Maybe you are surrounded with familiar role models who urge you forward by their own examples or expectations. Whatever the reason, when you go with the flow in your old life, you feel the force of momentum pushing you forward. But when you stop, gravity suddenly seems to grab hold of you, exerting a powerful force of inertia that immobilizes you with anxiety and fear.

Another reason that you may have a hard time biting off more than you can chew in pursuit of your desires is the power of expectation. Often late bloomers allow the power of other people's expectations to fuel their lives. A desire to please and the fear of failing others may be so intense that you regularly attempt—and achieve—extremely difficult tasks in order to fulfill external expectations. Or perhaps you are driven by expectations that you created for yourself years ago and have long outgrown. You may still be trying to prove yourself against standards that no longer even matter to you. Or you may find that the expectations you created for yourself years ago have multiplied and a whole colony of people now share them (including your Chorus of No).

Something that you may have forgotten is that *you* played a large role in creating that momentum and set of expectations in the first place, and *you* have the power to create momentum in a new direction and to forge fresh expectations. One of the best ways to do this is to bite off more than you can chew. The experience of Cynthia, a late-blooming restaurateur, provides an excellent example of this advice at work.

When Cynthia graduated from high school, she applied to a temporary employment agency and took the first job she was offered—a month-long assignment with a local shipping company. The fact that Cynthia knew nothing about shipping did not deter her from accepting—and excelling at—the job. When the temporary assignment was over, Cynthia was hired as a permanent employee. She learned every aspect of the business and within two years was promoted to a higher position in another state.

Cynthia accepted this promotion and once more excelled, acquiring greater and greater skills and becoming a highly valued, experienced employee. When the company she was working for went bankrupt, Cynthia was quickly recruited by a competing company. She continued to climb in her field, accepting promotions and, at one point, even initiating a move to a foreign office. After twenty-two years of excelling in the shipping field, fulfilling and even exceeding the expectations of her employers, Cynthia lost her job through a corporate restructuring. Although she walked away with a generous "golden parachute" that guaranteed her a full year to find a new job, Cynthia was overwhelmed by fear each time she imagined starting a new career.

For the first time in her adult life, neither the momentum of her initial career decision nor the high expectations of her employers were pushing her forward. In reality, Cynthia's own capacity for hard work, her good business sense, and her creative problem-solving skills were the secrets of her success. Yet, without the structure of expectation and the momentum of her past success, she felt immobilized as she contemplated launching a new career as a restaurateur—a career that had been quietly calling to her for years. Finally, as the year she had given herself to find a new job drew to a close, Cynthia realized that she had to act. Pushing aside her fear, she signed on the dotted line and acquired a lease on a restaurant property, which she soon transformed into the thriving Café Cynthia.

"I knew I had no experience in this industry," Cynthia recalled. "I saw no reason why I should succeed in it—I knew the failure rate of restaurants. But I felt that if I didn't take this risk now, in my early forties, I would never take it. If I was going to do it, I had to do it now. I was terrified every step of the way, but the decision to open the restaurant created its own momentum. Once I got caught up in it, I didn't even have time to worry about whether or not I was doing the right thing. Sometimes it only takes that one act of courage to get you off home base. Before long, you find yourself running to first base, and then to second, and there is no turning back."

By overcoming her anxiety long enough to actually acquire the business that was calling out to her, Cynthia invested herself—her time, her money, and even her reputation—in her own success. Once she created the expectation that she would succeed, and established a new momentum (fueled by her investment), there was no turning back. Cynthia no longer found herself wondering whether or not she could be a restaurateur. She *was* a restaurateur, and all the energy that had hitherto been spent on wondering and worrying was translated into hard work that promoted her success.

Biting off more than you can chew is a strategy that can help you to translate the mental leap of faith imagined in the previous chapter into solid, purposeful action. Once you become clear about what you want to do, and have done some basic planning to prepare the way, you must just go ahead and do it. By taking actions that translate your desire into reality, you will find that you build new momentum and create new expectations that will hurry you toward your ultimate goal.

Sometimes you can take that big bite by acting privately on a commitment you have made, like starting to write a novel (instead of just thinking about it), buying a book about a new career, or taking some other quiet action. However, it is all too easy to cheat if the action you take does not involve either a significant investment of internal resources or the powerful pressure of external expectations. Biting off more than you can chew is a strategy that invites you to use what you know about yourself and why you perform well in certain situations, and apply those same pressures to your new goals. You can harness both your strengths and your so-called character defects in order to overcome the biggest challenges that lie between your life as it is and your vision for the future.

Are you incredibly stubborn once you say you are going to do something? Then declare that you intend to succeed at your vision. Do you like to please others? Then make sure one or more people are expecting you to succeed. Do you hate to be wrong? Then don't be afraid to let the people whom you most want to impress, or prove something to, know what you are doing. Are you compulsively organized, just as long as you have a deadline and a goal? Then set up a structure within which you know you will perform.

In the following exercise, you will analyze the secrets of your past successes and identify the circumstances that have called forth your most courageous achievements. Then you will imagine ways to create similar circumstances in order to push and pull yourself through the challenging actions that are required to translate your vision for the future into a real and satisfying life. Once you identify these strategies, you can plan the ideal time to use them. One word of advice: Don't take these actions yet! Plan them thoughtfully now, and I can promise that you will have a much greater chance of succeeding when the time is right.

EXERCISES

Exercise: Learning from the past

1. Think back over the times in your life when you have succeeded in overcoming really difficult challenges. These challenges may have come in the form of academic achievements, athletic victories, artistic accomplishments, acquisition of professional skills, relationships to which you have devoted your time and efforts, spiritual quandaries that you have overcome, or physical or mental illnesses from which you have recovered or with which you have learned to live creatively.

2. As you review these past challenges, ask yourself what made it possible for you to deal with them (see the example and worksheet provided). What were the secrets of your past successes? What combination of personality quirks and external circumstances contributed to these achievements?

   For example, did you find that you consistently overcame challenges because it was simply expected that you would, like Cynthia? Did having a partner, mentor, or role model make it much easier to learn new skills or overcome obstacles? Was your success fueled by the desire to prove that you were right, or that someone else was wrong? Did you succeed when you humbled yourself and relied upon faith in a higher power to pull you through? Did you perform well when you knew that others would be excited or pleased by your work?

3. Now, return your thoughts to the meditation you completed in the previous chapter. Which challenges separating your present life from your vision of the future caused

you the most anxiety? At what point in the meditation did you find yourself stopped in your tracks, overwhelmed by fear or anxiety? Which necessary step seemed to present a large stumbling block to your progress? Problem steps might include actions like quitting jobs, going back to school, or applying to schools. A big stumbling block for me was making time in my life for writing before it could make money or earn me praise.

4. Now, write down a few ideas about how you can trick yourself into biting off more than you can chew. Come up with a strategy that will help you to overcome this hurdle, based upon what you know about yourself and your past success. This strategy will increase your comfort, strengthen your commitment, and intensify your determination to succeed. If you find it too difficult to plan this out ahead of time, then wait until you actually bump up against this challenge and use this exercise to help you deal with it.

For example, I was a perennial people-pleaser, so when it came to making time for my desire to become a writer, I needed to create a situation in which people expected me to write, and write well. There weren't any publishers sitting around waiting for me to submit a book proposal, so I invited a friend to join me as a partner in writing a book proposal. This friend was incredibly efficient, organized, and deadline-oriented. We mapped out our schedule together, deciding when our proposal would be completed and who would do what. We also agreed to meet regularly to compare notes and measure our progress. Suddenly, someone else was expecting me to write. The anxiety I felt about whether or not I was up to the task of writing a successful book proposal was outweighed by my desire not to disappoint my friend's expectations. As a result, we completed our proposal on schedule and even succeeded in finding an agent to represent the book.

I hope this exercise has reminded you of your past achievements and the secrets that underlaid them. Undoubtedly, you have already met significant challenges in the course of your life. Surely you have mastered new skills and overcome various shortcomings, fulfilling, and even exceeding, the expectations others (and even you) had for yourself. Now that you have dared to describe the great expectations you have for your future, let the memory of these past achievements propel you forward. As you prepare to live your new life, get ready to bite off more than you can chew—over and over again. You may be surprised to discover how sweet and easy success is to digest.

EXAMPLE

Exercise: Learning from the past

In this exercise, you will recall the times when you have succeeded in overcoming difficult challenges and learn how you can apply the secrets of your past successes to future challenges.

1. Describe two or three major challenges or significant achievements you have accomplished in the past.
   getting my real estate license
   juggling part-time work with raising two young children

2. What elements contributed to your past success? Include external forces (e.g., other people's expectations, financial incentive), internal forces (e.g., fear of failure, desire to please), personality traits (e.g., willfulness, competitiveness), and supports (e.g., prayer, therapy, mentors).

   External forces _need to make money, desire to look successful_

   Internal forces _drive to succeed_

   Personality traits _well-organized, ambitious, energetic_

   Supports _network of working mothers, prayer group, yoga, and meditation_

3. Revisit the meditation you completed in the previous chapter and briefly describe the challenge(s) or achievement(s) that give you the most anxiety as you move toward your new vision of success.
   trying to make money by selling my artwork
   juggling painting, real estate, and demands of my family

4. Considering what has worked for you in the past, suggest strategies you can use to overcome this (these) hurdle(s). Be sure to harness external and internal forces, capitalize upon your personality traits, and build in the supports you need to succeed.

1. Give up a portion of real estate work in order to create a financial incentive to make money from my artwork (and provide time to pursue art career).

2. Find a support network of other artists to help me focus my energy, solve problems, and be accountable; share my concerns with my prayer group.

3. Let others know that I am trying to become a professional artist; create the expectation that I will succeed and then work hard to fulfill it.

4. Use prayer and meditation to center me in my artwork. Focus my ambition, organizational skills, and energy on my new career.

WORKSHEET

Exercise: Learning from the past

In this exercise, you will recall the times when you have succeeded in overcoming difficult challenges and learn how you can apply the secrets of your past successes to future challenges.

1. Describe two or three major challenges or significant achievements you have accomplished in the past.

_____

_____

_____

2. What elements contributed to your past success? Include external forces (e.g., other people's expectations, financial incentive), internal forces (e.g., fear of failure, desire to please), personality traits (e.g., willfulness, competitiveness), and supports (e.g., prayer, therapy, mentors).

   External forces _____

   _____

   Internal forces _____

   _____

   Personality traits _____

   _____

   Supports _____

   _____

3. Revisit the meditation you completed in the previous chapter and briefly describe the challenge(s) or achievement(s) that give you the most anxiety as you move toward your new vision of success.

_____

_____

_____

4. Considering what has worked for you in the past, suggest strategies you can use to overcome this (these) hurdle(s). Be sure to harness external and internal forces, capitalize upon your personality traits, and build in the supports you need to succeed.

_____
_____
_____
_____
_____
_____
_____
_____
_____
_____
_____
_____
_____
_____
_____
_____
_____
_____
_____
_____
_____
_____
_____
_____
_____
_____
_____
_____

CHAPTER 8

Fifth Principle of Unconventional Wisdom

Count Your Chickens Before They're Hatched

Why is it that so many figures of speech that farmers have handed down to us urge caution and even pessimism, while those from sports figures recommend faith and optimism? "Don't count your chickens before they're hatched." I can almost see the pursed lips of a dour old farmer doling out this bit of gloomy advice as his young daughter rushes back breathlessly from the chicken coop with the news that many, many chicks will soon emerge. Listening to her father, the young girl's entire worldview shifts. The world is no longer pregnant with possibility. Fertilized eggs may not bear life.

Dreams may not unfold. Hopes should probably not be breathlessly, faithfully announced. We should not joyfully anticipate the outcome we desire. Instead, we should carefully prepare ourselves for the worst.

Now imagine this same little girl with a different father, a sports coach who has urged numerous children to try their best on the playing field. "I'm going to win the race tomorrow!" she announces to her father as she jogs along beside him. Will he prepare his daughter to deal with possible failure, or suggest that she should be ready to settle for less than first place? Not likely. "Keep your eye on the prize and do the best you can," is what he'd probably say. "Think like a winner! Go for the gold! Beat your personal best!" These are the words of advice that come to us from the realm of sports.

Of course, I can understand the reasoning behind the farmer's cautious advice. Nature does not always cooperate with our plans. There is a good chance that one or two chicks actually will not hatch. But why shouldn't you at least allow yourself to imagine the prospect that all the eggs will bear warm, new life? Aren't you likely to tend to your dreams all the more carefully if you believe that every single dream has the potential to bear fruit? And, in the meantime, won't you enjoy a few delicious moments of anticipation as you imagine the many rewards you will enjoy when your dreams come true?

Count your chickens before they're hatched is the fifth principle of unconventional wisdom for two reasons. The first is that this revised adage reminds you to have faith in and remain aware of the abundance in the world. It is absolutely essential that you keep your mind focused on the rewards you will receive when your life change begins to pay off. You need to count the not-so-far-off gifts that will result from your acts of self-transformation *and* to recognize the daily rewards that will come along as soon as you begin the journey. Only by doing so can you find the drive and the enthusiasm you will need to make the sacrifices and take the risks that will be required along the way.

Anyone in the field of business will tell you that there is nothing like the lure of concrete incentives to motivate a workforce. What rewards can you look forward to reaping as soon as you begin to actively pursue your vision? Will you love the work you do? Will you earn more money? Will you have more leisure time? Are you counting the days until you can stop going to the office and start working at home? Then focus your attention and your imagination on what you have to gain on every level—material, emotional, and spiritual—and you will find yourself springing forward into the future, fueled with impatience and enthusiasm.

And while you're at it, try to stop worrying so much about what you have to lose. If you listen to those fears, you are much more likely to succumb to anxiety and procrastination, to give up easily, or to settle for less than you want. In fact, each time you find yourself spending five minutes obsessing about what might go wrong, make yourself spend an equal amount of time dreaming about what can go right.

The second reason I encourage you to count your chickens before they're hatched is that you need to be realistic, as well as enthusiastic, about the life you are planning. You need to make sure you are setting a truly desirable and attainable goal. This principle invites you to use a tool borrowed from the business world called *cost/benefit analysis* to measure the rewards and the sacrifices of the new life you want. The story of Peter, a late bloomer who made a career change from the legal profession to the culinary arts world when he was in his fifties, provides an excellent example of the wisdom of counting your chickens before they're hatched, both as an incentive and as preparation for change.

Peter loved food and eating out at restaurants when he was a little boy, but it never occurred to him to pursue cooking as a profession. "I didn't know any nice Jewish boys who were chefs," he laughs. Instead, his childhood role models were the fictional television lawyer Perry Mason, and a real-life uncle who was a lawyer. As a child, Peter received a lot of positive feedback when he said he wanted to be a lawyer. As an adult, the positive reinforcement continued, but Peter began to notice that it was a little one-sided. "My parents asked questions like 'What's your title?' and 'How much money are you making?'" Peter remembers. "Nobody ever asked me if I enjoyed what I was doing."

The challenges and rewards of being a lawyer were satisfying to Peter for twenty years, but after a while the job began to feel like a grind, especially when his focus shifted to divorce law. "It was becoming harder and harder to go to work," he said. "I knew I was doing a good job for my clients, but I wasn't pleased with what I did. I didn't enjoy the conflict anymore. Emotionally, it was very wearing. There was nothing exciting about it except the paycheck." Peter also said that he had very little balance in his life, with little time or energy left for leisure or interests outside of work.

When Peter's stepchildren left home, making both a geographic move and financial downsizing feasible, he saw his opportunity to make a change. For a long time, he had felt his early interest in fine restaurants and gourmet food growing into a more insistent calling. Friends had always noticed that the one hobby Peter made time for in his life was entertaining and cooking delicious meals. Now he began to explore ways to turn this pleasurable pastime into something more than a hobby. He started taking Fridays off to cater lunch for his wife and her friends and to work in a friend's restaurant. The rewards of cooking professionally were clearly gratifying. "I loved the cooking," Peter recalls. "It was great when people enjoyed the food I made and said, 'You're a good cook.'"

After reading an article about cooking schools, Peter allowed himself to envision giving up his legal career to go back to school and start anew. The prospect of giving up the demands of his old life, moving to a new city, and learning a whole new, pleasurable set of skills was very exciting and enticing. But even as he allowed himself to imagine these future rewards, he also considered the demands (being a line chef convinced him he didn't want to work in a restaurant), the options (he learned about being a private chef), and the sacrifices he would have to make (giving up a second car).

"I did the numbers," said Peter, who, along with his wife, didn't want their finances to change significantly. They realized that by selling their house for a profit and moving to a city with a lower cost of living, they could rely upon a combination of investments and Peter's reduced salary to maintain a similar standard of living. Today, Peter says, "I am making a lot less money than I used to. I went from a very intense, stressful, well-paying profession to one in which I can control my time much more. I work three days a week. I get smiles from my clients, not tears. My work produces happiness. I have a much more enjoyable life, a mix of activities . . . balance."

Not surprisingly, Peter has two bits of advice to pass on to other late bloomers. They reflect his optimism and his caution. "Find something you like to do, and the money will follow," he says. "But remember, every career has its costs," he adds. "Do a life assessment, be deliberate, and research your options."

If you are ready to start taking concrete actions to change your life, this is a good time to assess both the benefits and the costs of doing so. There will undoubtedly be some sacrifices that you will have to make. But if you are clear ahead of time about what these are, and why you are willing to make them, you won't be unpleasantly surprised when they come up. Imagine what might have happened if Peter hadn't decided ahead of time that he was willing to take a big pay cut in order to enjoy his work and his life more, and if he hadn't planned to adjust his whole lifestyle accordingly. He might have scurried out of the kitchen and back to court as soon as he got his first paycheck—jumping out of the frying pan, right back into the fire.

Maybe you are one of the many late bloomers I have met who flip-flop back and forth between their old lives and their new ones for years. Perhaps you find that you never really get ahead because you just can't commit to the changes you have to make. As soon as you start to put your new life into place and experience some of the sacrifices that are involved, you hurry back to your old life—especially if the benefits of your new life haven't started to kick in yet. But once you get back to the familiar way of doing things, you remember why you wanted to give that way of life up. You start dreaming again about the rewards of the life you want to lead, and the cycle starts all over again.

That is why it is so important that you count your chickens before they're hatched by identifying both the rewards and the sacrifices your new life promises to bring *before* you set out to achieve it. Once you determine that you want the benefits of your new life (necessary sacrifices, and all) more than you want to continue to make do with the rewards of your old life, you will find that it is much harder to turn back. When the going gets rough, you will remember why you chose the path that you did, and this knowledge will help you stick to it. When you feel yourself slipping into regrets, wishing for old rewards that don't really have much value for you anymore, you will remember what does matter to you. If you can become clear about what rewards you really want, and what sacrifices you are willing to make for them, like Peter, you will be well prepared to handle the challenges you meet along the way toward the future of your dreams.

EXERCISES

Meditation: If I could change my life . . .

In this meditation and the exercise that follows, I invite you to create a list of the many benefits you will experience as you change your life, and to balance this list with a concrete accounting of the sacrifices you will have to make in order to get them. Begin by sitting quietly for a few moments and imagining what you would do if you were free to start changing your life *right now.*

1. What is the very first rewarding thing you would do? (The first thing I always imagine doing is unplugging the telephone!) How will you feel when you do this?

2. What other changes would you make? What might happen as a result? If you like, you can start by thinking about the obvious, practical things you will need to do (like going back to school or getting a part-time job). But don't forget to think about the fun things, too: for example, would you change the way you dress? And consider subtle little changes (perhaps you imagine yourself becoming more outspoken) and unexpected actions that you might take when you start to follow your dream (like sleeping late or dancing around the house when you wake up).

3. Think about all the good things that will come into your life as you begin to make these changes: pleasurable experiences, new people, revitalized energy levels, an improved sense of well-being, different activities, or more rewarding

ways of getting paid (whether you receive more money, or money you feel better about earning, or make less money but have more leisure time). What are the best possible rewards you can imagine receiving by making these changes in your life? Take plenty of time to enjoy thinking about these.

4. Whenever you feel overwhelmed by fear or anxiety about the changes you are making in the future, or feel tempted to turn back, return to this meditation. It is essential to remind yourself often of the rewards your efforts will earn—and to recognize them as soon as they come into your life!

Exercise: Cost/benefit analysis

1. Take a piece of paper and divide it into two vertical columns (see the example and worksheet provided). At the top of the left-hand column, write the word *Rewards*. At the top of the column on the right, write *Sacrifices*. Or use the worksheet in the book.

2. List the rewards you imagine reaping as you actively pursue your new vision in the left-hand column. Be sure to include spiritual and emotional rewards as well as the physical and material benefits you will gain (see the example provided for ideas on how to do this).

3. Now, try to imagine what costs or sacrifices will be required in order to gain the rewards you just described. Make a list of these in the right-hand column under the heading *Sacrifices*. If certain rewards require specific sacrifices, write those down across from each other as shown in

the example. Not every reward will have a cost associated with it, but whenever it does, write it down on the appropriate line.

4. Finally, consider what other sacrifices you might have to make in order to change your life. Add what comes to mind to your list. Are there any rewards that you forgot to list that balance these sacrifices? If so, add them in the appropriate places.

When you have completed your list of rewards and sacrifices, read it over again. Count the many benefits that await you. Then measure these against the sacrifices that will be involved. Does this sound like a life that you would like to lead? My guess is that your review will leave you feeling even more eager to get started, since you will have allowed yourself to consider all the good things that lie ahead. Whenever you feel tempted to give up your dream, spend some time considering the rewards you have listed. These will help to remind you of the many gifts that will come when you are true to yourself and your vision for the future. When you feel anxious about the changes you must make and the risks involved, reread the sacrifices you have listed. You can reassure yourself that you have thought it all through and you will just need to persevere. The life you want to live, with all its complex gifts and costs, awaits. Just don't keep it waiting too much longer!

Exercise: Cost/benefit analysis

Following the instructions for this exercise, describe the *Rewards* (benefits) and *Sacrifices* (costs) that are associated with pursuing your vision for the future.

Rewards	Sacrifices
I will feel like I am finally answering my calling as an artist; I will no longer feel like I am ignoring a vital part of myself.	I will have to make an investment of time and money in following this calling: give up free time and luxuries like extra meals out and new clothes.
I will no longer hate going to my real estate job since I will feel like it is a means to an end—supporting my developing career as an artist—and since I will be doing it part-time.	I will have to be patient while I make a gradual transition to becoming a full-time artist; I will probably feel torn in two pieces for a while.
I will feel like I am being more honest about who I am; I will feel like I am asking the world to honor and respect my true talents and interests.	My boss and co-workers at the real estate company may feel inconvenienced and may give me a hard time; my friends might think I'm flaky; my parents will worry about my finances.
I'll meet new people who will share my passion for art.	I may find that some of my old friends don't support this change and I may lose some friends.

Rewards	Sacrifices
I'll have a new sense of excitement about working and living; I'll feel the potential of getting out of what feels like a dead-end career and exploring something new and fulfilling.	I will feel some anxieties about earning money as an artist as well as fear that I'm not really good—something that most artists probably contend with regularly.
I will rekindle my childhood love of painting and drawing and express myself creatively in my work and life.	I will work longer hours for less pay as I start from scratch as a professional artist; I may have to work years before I can reach my old salary level, but in the long run, I may find that I can earn more and really enjoy what I am doing with my life.

133

Exercise: Cost/benefit analysis

Following the instructions for this exercise, describe the *Rewards* (benefits) and *Sacrifices* (costs) that are associated with pursuing your vision for the future.

Rewards	Sacrifices

Rewards	Sacrifices

CHAPTER 9

Sixth Principle of Unconventional Wisdom

Put All Your Eggs in One Basket

"I'm putting all my eggs in one basket," is the refrain of a jaunty song written by Irving Berlin in 1936. "I'm betting everything I've got on you," continue his optimistic lyrics, which celebrate the joyful pursuit of love despite the risk of disappointment. This is the theme song for late bloomers who allow themselves to fall headlong in love with the lives they want to lead. At a certain point in this love affair, you too will need to go on and throw caution to the wind. You must embrace your new life wholeheartedly and give it your all—all your energy, all your passion, all your faith, and all (or nearly all) of your resources. You must engage completely with your new life and say "I do" before a cloud of witnesses, including the naysayers inside your head, and the real ones outside it as well. Once you do so, you will be swept along by the power of your new life: one that is fueled by desire, and that celebrates all that you most cherish about yourself and the world.

"Don't put all your eggs in one basket" is another one of those cautious admonitions that come to us from farmers. These pessimistic words of advice stem from the fear that if you put all your eggs into one basket and drop it, you might lose a whole day's harvest. It is indeed good stewardship to avoid foolishly putting fragile resources at risk. But if you did put all your eggs into one basket, wouldn't you carry that basket very, very carefully? And if worse came to worse and you tripped, dropping the basket and breaking all the eggs, wouldn't there be more eggs to gather tomorrow?

During your late bloomer transformation, a point will come when you will need to put all your eggs into one basket. Until you are prepared to invest all your resources in pursuit of your life dream, you will always be leaving some part of yourself behind. Instead of focusing your full attention upon completing the journey ahead of you, you will constantly be glancing over your shoulder making sure that what you have left behind (a job you no longer like, an empty relationship, an unsatisfying career path) is still there. In the back of your mind you will think that, should you fail in your new endeavor, you could always turn around and go back. However, your efforts to keep these backup positions in place, once they are no longer really needed, can actually undermine your purposeful single-mindedness, and divide your resources as you try to move ahead. As Berlin put it, "too many irons in the fire is worse than not having any."

While it may be a good idea to divide your energies for a while, and build up new resources while protecting your old ones, at a certain point you need to "go for broke." The image of ballast provides a helpful metaphor for understanding this idea. Ships that are going to pick up new cargo are often filled with ballast, heavy material which balances the otherwise empty ship as it makes its way to port. This ballast is essential to the safe completion of the journey's first leg, but once the ship arrives at the new port and is prepared for new cargo, the old ballast must be unloaded. If the ship were to fill up with new cargo in addition to its old ballast, it would surely sink. But with its ballast unloaded and its new cargo stored beneath the hull, the ship is prepared for a safe journey to its next destination.

You will need to recognize the point at which you have safely reached the harbor and can unload the ballast of your old ways of being—outgrown jobs, old ways of relating to people, stale emotions, bankrupt belief systems—and fill yourself up with new, precious cargo. Certainly, there is always the risk that a seafaring vessel will sink, yet most shipping companies still load each ship to capacity before sending it on to the next port of call. You won't find many companies that adhere to a policy of putting only half of their cargo on board. This example from the life of a late bloomer illustrates this point.

Susan enjoyed a long, varied, and often satisfying career as a minister. She received a degree in divinity from Harvard University and held a variety of pastoral positions, ranging from parish minister to hospital chaplain. Yet as her career evolved, she kept feeling that something was missing from her work, a connection with a creative impulse which she had not yet learned to tap or fully express. In her late thirties, she tried to find more creative ways of working as a minister, and so she established an independent pastoral counseling practice focusing upon issues of work, life, relationships, and spirituality. But after a while, she realized that the creativity welling up inside of her demanded even more direct, physical expression. Soon after she turned forty, Susan cut her counseling work back to half-time and began taking art classes. "I told myself, 'I'll take these art classes and continue my current work and see what happens,'" she recalls. "At that point, I put about a half-dozen eggs in my basket."

At first, Susan was unsure whether this introduction to the arts would lead to a new hobby, to be pursued during her free time, or whether it would prove to be the first step toward a whole new career. She also felt a little nervous about the changes she was making, fearful that others wouldn't understand such a significant change of course, or that they might think her new interests were frivolous. But the more deeply she became engaged in her study of art, the more Susan's interests blossomed and her talents emerged. As this happened, she found it harder and harder to invest herself wholeheartedly in her counseling practice, even working part-time. "Trying to continue half in and half out of that work began to deplete my resources. The emotional energy that my old work required was rising for me and was actually preventing me from pursuing an interest I really was excited about. When I did the cost/benefit analysis, I realized that keeping one foot in my old work was only holding me back from following my new sense of calling."

During this transitional period, Susan began to grow clear about a new career direction that was calling to her: the field of textile design. Even though she didn't yet know the exact nature of the career she would forge in this field, she realized that the time had come to divest her energies from her previous work and to devote all her resources to developing her new interest. "When I arrived at that moment of clarity, the realization that this was what I wanted my life to be about, I knew that I had to declare myself ready and committed," Susan said. "When I know what the next step in my life is, I find that I must take it fully, even if I don't know what the step after that will be. I have to trust that there will be a new momentum and believe that things will open up for me."

Once Susan acknowledged this moment of clarity, she set a date to retire from counseling. She fulfilled her remaining obligations and turned down future work. She also began planning a total immersion in her new interests, with the goal of establishing a sustainable career within two years—a career that might even weave in threads of her previous work. "Once I had made this decision," Susan concluded, "I found it easy to say, 'I'm no longer doing that,' without much explanation or apology. It felt good, setting that identity aside, clearing that work away. When I looked at my calendar, it was amazingly empty, and I thought, 'Now I get to plan my life around this new adventure,' and it was thrilling."

When you begin the journey from your old life toward the new pursuits you want to follow, like Susan, you will eventually arrive at a point of no return. As you begin to invest your creative energies and tangible resources in your vision for the future, the vision will begin to exert a powerful pull. New forces of momentum will propel you in directions different from those dictated by your old life. New rewards will accrue. New enthusiasms will bubble up. New energies will flow. Yet you may find yourself clinging to aspects of your old life even though you know that they not only no longer work for you, they also no longer fit with the new identity you are forging, and are even holding you back just when you need to be moving boldly forward.

You will probably find that the cost of clinging to these old ways gets higher every day: You might not be able to stand the person you become when you arrive at work; perhaps you will find yourself cringing each time the telephone rings, and dreading each new day that dawns. Maybe you will find that you can't perform very well in roles and activities that once came easily. You might start to lose interest, procrastinate, and make mistakes. Perhaps you will worry that you aren't very good at your old job anymore or that you might even get fired before you have a chance to quit. You may feel as if you are leading a double life, with two warring identities exhausting you by their struggle for dominance. When you arrive at this point, you will find that the energy you are spending to hold on to the past is actually depleting the resources you need to move ahead.

This is the point at which you need to go ahead and put all your eggs in one basket and travel toward the future without looking back. It is hard to predict exactly when you will arrive at this juncture. If you have a high tolerance for risk, you will be ready to do this fairly early on in your transformation. Out on a tightrope without a safety net in place, you may actually be fueled by the adrenaline rush that comes when you put your life on the line. If you are more cautious by nature, you may choose to wait until you feel that the new path you are forging is clear and relatively risk-free. You may wisely predict that you would not be able or willing to tolerate the anxiety that high-risk situations trigger. However, even the most risk-averse late bloomers must at some point be willing to close some doors before they can open other ones. This is the only way that you will be able to leave your past behind and move boldly and freely into the future you most desire.

EXERCISES

Meditation and Exercise: Are you ready?

Once you are actively engaged in your transition from old ways of being to new ones, you will need to take some time to think about the questions given below. By answering them honestly and thoughtfully, you can determine as best as possible whether you are ready to put all your eggs in one basket. As you work through this meditation, you may want to record some of your thoughts for future reference (see the example and worksheet provided).

1. Are you aware of any actions that you take that no longer feel comfortable or appropriate? Think about the obligations that you once fulfilled easily, but now face with dread or a heavy sense of unease. Are there occasions during which your life feels like a charade? Do you feel you have to assume a false identity in order to show up for certain tasks or deal with certain people? Conjure up these situations in your mind and feel the friction, the anxiety, and the negative energy that they create.

2. Now think about the times when you are actively pursuing your new interests and how you feel when you do this. Do you feel vitally engaged? Do you love the person you become when you engage with life in this new way? Can you imagine living your whole life this way? Feel the powerful sense of flow, the serenity, and the positive energy you experience when you imagine devoting yourself fully to your new vision.

3. Are the activities and demands you imagined in response to the first set of questions actually preventing you from fulfilling those envisioned in response to the second? Do you feel that you are actually sapping the energy you need for your new life by still investing in the old one? Do you feel divided against yourself? Try to identify the conflicting personalities and desires within you that are wearing you down through their struggle for power.

4. Can you imagine letting go of the activities and ways of being you described in your answers to the first question? Are you ready to accept the sacrifices involved? This might

be a good time to reread the exercise you completed in the previous chapter.

5. Can you imagine giving yourself over completely to the pursuit of your new vision? Can you see that by fully devoting yourself to this new life, you will be able to win the rewards it promises sooner rather than later? Can you see how you are actually holding yourself back by clinging to the past?

6. Are you ready to put all your eggs into one basket? Can you set a date in the not-so-distant future at which point you can bring your past ways of working, or being, to a close and throw open the door to your new life? What actions will you need to take in order to do this? Do you feel prepared to begin taking these actions now?

If your answer to this last question is yes, then write your "retirement date" in your calendar and schedule the actions you will need to take in order to keep this appointment with your new life. If your answer is "not yet," don't worry. Be patient and watchful. Soon, you will experience that moment of clarity—and you will know, without a doubt, that you can no longer do some things anymore, nor can you wait any longer to do other things. Both the force of your desire for the life you want to lead and the sheer energy that this desire unleashes will make it possible for you to leave your old life behind without regret.

Meditation and Exercise: Are you ready?

As you complete the meditation, you may wish to write down some of your thoughts using the following format.

1. Describe the increasingly uncomfortable actions, obligations, and situations you feel you are outgrowing, yet still engage in regularly (or even occasionally):

   Acting like the real estate know-it-all; volunteering to help people find or sell houses as soon as I meet them; trying to impress my boss by being the best agent on the team; blowing off steam by shopping, when I should be drawing or painting; sitting around and brooding about how frustrating my life is and thinking that I will never be able to find happiness or fulfillment.

2. What are some of the activities and situations you engage in, or imagine engaging in, when you devote yourself to your new vision?

   Being alone in my studio, painting, listening to music, feeling at peace with myself and full of energy and enthusiasm for my work; meeting new people and telling them that I am an artist, not a real estate agent; offering to paint a picture of someone's house instead of offering to sell it; getting up in the morning and meditating about how I can spend the day answering my calling as an artist.

3. How are the activities you described in answer to question 1 actually preventing you from fulfilling those actions you described in response to question 2?

   As long as I continue creating the expectation at work that I am going to be a driven, competitive real estate agent, I will have to work like one, which means not having free time to work on my art career. As long as I act like a realtor when I meet new people, people (including me) will expect me to be a realtor instead of an artist. As long as I brood about how unhappy I am, I will not have the energy or faith I need to find new happiness in a new career.

4. List the actions you need to take in order to let go of the outgrown activities and obligations you described and embrace the new ones you envisioned.

1. Set up my studio in the guest room and start spending time there.

2. Meditate every morning in order to focus positive energy on my art career.

3. Talk to my boss about going to work part-time in order to have time to paint.

4. Tell people who ask me what I do that I am an artist first, and realtor second.

5. Are you ready to put all your eggs in one basket? Set a date in the near future when you can start taking the actions you described in your answer to question 4. When can you get started?

This week!

WORKSHEET

Meditation and Exercise: Are you ready?

As you complete the meditation, you may want to write down some of your thoughts using the following format.

1. Describe the increasingly uncomfortable actions, obligations, and situations you feel you are outgrowing, yet still engage in regularly (or even occasionally):

_____

_____

_____

_____

_____

_____

2. What are some of the activities and situations you engage in, or imagine engaging in, when you devote yourself to your new vision?

_____

_____

_____

_____

_____

_____

3. How are the activities you described in answer to question 1 actually preventing you from fulfilling those actions you described in response to question 2?

_____

_____

_____

_____

_____

_____

4. List the actions you need to take in order to let go of the outgrown activities and obligations you described and embrace the new ones you envisioned.

_____

_____

_____

_____

_____

_____

_____

_____

_____

_____

5. Are you ready to put all your eggs in one basket? Set a date in the near future when you can start taking the actions you described in your answer to question 4. When can you get started?

_____

CHAPTER 10

Seventh Principle of Unconventional Wisdom

Ignore the Danger Signals

Like most people, you have probably been taught to recognize and respond appropriately to a whole host of danger signals. When someone honks a horn, you look up and down the road for threats. In school, you practiced evacuation procedures during mock fire alarms. Radio signals remind you to keep an ear out for weather updates and emergency procedures during storms. You learned early on what cats look like when they are ready to pounce and what sounds dogs make when their intentions are unfriendly. You have been trained to scan your environment constantly for signals that can help you to avoid danger, and you have probably learned these lessons very

149

well. Unfortunately, your trained responses can lead you astray when you venture out into new and untried territory, which is why late bloomers need to learn to ignore the danger signals from time to time.

Having spent much of my adult life in a crowded city with a high crime rate, I learned to be very wary when I was alone at night on a quiet, dark street. This response was healthy and quite sensible in the city. But when I spent a week camping in the wilderness, the anxiety that inevitably descended upon me as soon as the sun set over the lonely mountains made me the laughingstock of my companions. I was convinced that muggers lurked behind every tree, and suffered paroxysms of fear when a herd of elk drew near to graze in the moonlight. On that vacation, I learned that my alarm system could easily misfire, triggering an intense—and inappropriate—anxiety response, especially when I pushed the boundaries of my experiences and bush-whacked into unknown territory.

When you embark upon your journey of life change, you will begin to hear alarms that warn you that danger is near. As you cast off old roles, break obsolete rules, abandon familiar habits, and forge new paths, you will find yourself continually receiving misinformation from your inner voices, as well as from those without, all warning you to turn back, to avoid risk, and be fearful of change. While your past life was most likely shaped by carefully heeding such warning signals, your future happiness will depend upon your willingness to turn a deaf ear to these danger signals and to endure the temporary discomfort that will result. The story of Lily's challenging, but ultimately successful transition from working as a copywriter at an advertising agency to becoming a freelance journalist provides a perfect example.

"I was always a people-pleaser," Lily confesses. "It was almost as if I had a second sense. I knew what people wanted to hear, and I knew how to say it. In fact, I was actually afraid *not* to say it." Clearly this was a great trait to harness in the field of advertising. Combined with her talent as a writer, this trait fueled Lily's successful career as the creator of appealing and effective advertising copy. But once the thrill of succeeding in this career wore off, and Lily found herself working sixty-hour weeks to prove herself to her boss and her clients, the words she wrote seemed increasingly meaningless to her, and she burned out. She felt the stirrings of her longstanding desire to be a journalist becoming more insistent, and she longed to write meaningful articles about topics that mattered to her. Yet fearful of making a change, she clung to her job with its regular salary, benefits, and prestige. Then one day she read an article on a subject that she had long been passionate about, which turned out to have been written by a college classmate of hers.

"I was furious," Lily recalled. "Furious at my classmate for beating me to the punch, furious at myself for holding back, and furious that I was so jealous." Lily's anger served as a catalyst, driving her to take actions she had been postponing for years. She quickly did some math and figured out that by cashing in a portion of her savings, she would have enough money to quit her job and pursue a new career in freelance journalism for one year. Yet as soon as she mustered enough courage to quit her job—an action she described as "a people-pleaser's nightmare"—Lily became overwhelmed by anxiety.

The fear that no one would be interested in her personal opinions crippled Lily when she sat down to write her first article. An older sibling's childhood refrain, "Nobody cares about what you think," echoed in her ears as she tried to draft query letters to editors regarding subjects she was interested in. A surprising number of family members and acquaintances repeated another unwelcome refrain when Lily declared her intention to become a writer: "Writers don't make any money." Even though she knew a number of self-supporting writers, Lily anxiously pored over the want ads every Sunday, considering job opportunities in the field she had abandoned, because she feared it might prove to be the only way to support herself in the end.

"I realized that I had been hearing these intensely negative messages for years and believing them," Lily recalled. "The hardest thing I had to do was to ignore them. It was harder than getting editors to talk to me, harder than writing, and harder than getting published. By making changes in my life—changes I had been dying to make for years—I was challenging all the fears I had internalized over the years," Lily added. "I was breaking all the rules, and it terrified me."

Lily's fears often caused her to procrastinate when it came to pitching new story ideas to editors, and triggered a bad case of writer's block when she sat down to compose articles. When her old advertising agency asked her back to work on a freelance basis, Lily jumped at the opportunity. "It was so much easier to give in to the voices that said I couldn't succeed at what I really wanted to do," she recalled. "But after a few months, I couldn't stand doing the advertising work, even part-time, and I had to quit all over again." This time, when Lily tried to focus her energies upon her writing career, she began to experience panic attacks that lasted for days at a time. Rather than give in to her anxiety, she scheduled an appointment with a psychiatrist and began a combination of therapy and medication to help her handle it.

"I knew that these fears were irrational. Once I found a way to calm them down, I was able to do the work I really wanted to do." Within six months of beginning her treatment for the panic attacks, Lily was able not only to end her therapy and stop taking the medication, but also to focus productively on her new career. She began to sell magazine articles, and even to write a book, something her past anxiety levels had prevented her from doing. "Now, when my old fears crop up," Lily explains, "I realize that it doesn't really mean that the world is about to crash down on me and that I need to run and hide. It just means that I am afraid—and I have learned that I can deal with that."

The danger signals you will experience when you begin to change your life may include panic and anxiety attacks, spells of depression, or undirected anger. Even though you may be able to determine that these responses are in fact irrational, they can still send you running in the opposite direction, convinced that you must be doing something wrong if you feel so bad. More likely than not, these emotional states actually indicate that you are doing something right. When you challenge your old belief systems and start rocking the boat, an intensely agitated emotional state is likely to follow. Old demons may creep up on you; false assumptions may attempt to convince you of their truth; unwelcome voices may pipe up.

If you are committed to changing your life, you must make every effort to keep going and not turn back when you become uncomfortable. Instead, try to recognize and accept your emotional unease as a symptom of growth. If your symptoms are fairly mild, you can probably just resign yourself to temporary discomfort. If, however, you find that you are suffering from persistent depression, anxiety, panic attacks, or other forms of emotional fallout, like Lily did, you should seek professional guidance. You may even need to postpone further change until you regain an emotional comfort level—but you should not have to turn back.

Another kind of danger signal sneaks up on late bloomers like a wolf in sheep's clothing. These wily signals come not in the form of feelings, but rather in the guise of highly rational ideas. They may suggest that you postpone your pursuit of an insistent calling, compromise your ideals, or deny what you know deep down inside to be true about what you want from life. These ideas can send you scurrying back to a job you hate, a relationship you know is over, and a life that suffocates you. They are usually echoes of ideas you have heard over the years that have warped your true comprehension of your identity, your worth, and the world you live in.

It is often very hard to recognize these danger signals, since they come so well camouflaged as rational thoughts, but here is a good rule of thumb: Whenever you find yourself preparing to backtrack or backpedal, or whenever you feel yourself setting your sights too low or off to one side of the real mark, stop and ask yourself *why* you are preparing to settle for less. Before taking any action that will send you off in the wrong direction, you need to pause and identify the fears and assumptions that are driving your thoughts, and determine whether they apply to your new life, or are simply insistent reminders of the life you are leaving behind. I highly recommend that you create your own support network to aid you in this process—a network that can include trusted friends, colleagues on parallel paths, mentors or role models, and therapeutic professionals. Your friends and counselors are much less likely to be taken in by these disguised fears than you are.

When I recommend that you ignore some of the danger signals you'll encounter as you remake your life, what I really mean is that you should stop taking them at face value. You should not draw your hand back from the flames at the first sensation of heat, because what you are really experiencing is a fire that has the power to transform. You should not give in to immediate flight responses, retreating into the shell of your old life, whenever you experience emotional discomfort. Instead, you should get as close as possible to your fears in order to understand them better. You must learn to analyze and deconstruct the messages that flash through your mind and heart, by listening carefully to what they have to say. An occasional jolt of fear or shudder of anxiety is inevitable as you go about changing your life. You *are* rocking the boat. You *are* setting out on an unfamiliar path. You must learn to use your fears, not be ruled by them. By decoding outgrown fears and responding to them positively, you can turn them to your advantage. The following exercise will help you learn how to use your fears to propel yourself forward, instead of allowing them to hold you back.

EXERCISES

Exercise: Calling your fears by name

Whenever you begin to experience danger signals, whether they come in the form of twinges of anxiety or loud and clear messages that say, "Turn around and go back now!", I recommend that you stop and ask yourself, "What am I afraid of?" This simple discipline can save you years of frustration and misguided action. But why wait until fear strikes? If you start now, naming the fears and fallacies that once ruled your life, you will be better prepared to recognize these false alarms when they go off. In this exercise, I invite you to conjure up your vision of the life you want to lead and listen carefully to all the negative thoughts and anxieties that crop up.

1. As you think about changing your life, ask yourself, "What am I afraid of?" Jot down every single fear, whether rational or irrational, that comes to mind when you consider pursuing the future that beckons to you (see the example and worksheet provided).

2. Reread your list of fears and address them one at a time, asking, "Why am I afraid of this?" The answers that you write down will help you to identify the sources of your

false alarms. These might include past experiences that discouraged you, but are no longer relevant to your present life; misconceptions about you, your talents, or the world that were passed along to you by parents, siblings, teachers, or friends; real future challenges that you will need to deal with creatively; or pure, irrational emotions that you can recognize as such.

3. When put to the test, people often succeed in overcoming their fears. This can be the case in dealing with irrational fears and phobias, as well as with tangible dangers like fire, storm, or personal attack. People often discover that, when flight is no longer an option, they can successfully fight for their lives and prevail over seemingly insurmountable threats. Review each fear you named and ask yourself, "What would I do if this fear came true? How could I overcome it or deal with it?"

4. Finally, beneath each fear you have listed, write down a positive affirmation that addresses the fear. This statement might directly contradict the fear, or simply prove its irrelevance to your current situation. Make sure that this affirmation is a statement in which you can believe. For example, Lily's list of fears and matching affirmations included the following:

Fear: I'm afraid that I can't making a living as a writer.
Affirmation: Plenty of people support themselves as writers. So can I.

Fear: I'm afraid people won't like what I have to say.
Affirmation: What other people think about what I have to say doesn't matter as long as I know that I am telling the truth about what matters to me.

Fear: I'm afraid I will run out of money.

Affirmation: I have always figured out how to support myself up until now; I am sure I can support myself in the future.

These affirmations can help you respond to your fears with a faith that can speed you forward along the path to greater success and happiness. You may want to write these sentences on index cards or on a page in your daybook. Whenever you begin to feel overwhelmed by anxiety or feel the need for inspiration, you can reread your affirmations and go right ahead and ignore the danger signals.

Exercise: Calling your fears by name

Use this exercise to name your fears and formulate reassuring affirmations that can help you address these fears when they crop up.

Fear:

  I'm afraid that I won't be able to make a living as an artist.

Why I am afraid of this:

  My parents discouraged me from trying to make a living as an artist; so many people say that it is so hard, if not impossible, to do it.

How could I overcome this fear or deal with it, should the need arise?

  People told me it was hard to be a successful realtor, but I succeeded. I'll just have to work hard and study the art field, just like I did in real estate, and do my best. Also, I can always fall back on part-time real estate work to make ends meet if needed.

Positive affirmation that addresses or negates this fear:

  I believe that my talents and hard work will be rewarded, as they have been in the past.

Fear:

  I am afraid my boss won't like me anymore, and might even punish me if I reduce my commitment to real estate.

Why I am afraid of this:

  I have always been afraid that people won't like me and will punish me if I don't put their needs or interests first. It's an old pattern.

How could I overcome this fear or deal with it, should the need arise?

<u>If my boss does react this way, I can try to see this as a test for me to put myself first, no matter what the cost. If it gets too painful, I can talk to my therapist.</u>

Positive affirmation that addresses or negates this fear:

<u>Whether other people like me isn't as important as whether I like myself.</u>

Fear:

<u>I'm afraid I won't be any good as an artist.</u>

Why I am afraid of this:

<u>I've never given myself a chance to find out whether I am good or not; I've been taught to be afraid of my calling and to ignore my talents.</u>

How could I overcome this fear or deal with it, should the need arise?

<u>If I'm not satisfied with my skills at first, I can take classes, practice, and keep working until I achieve the level of ability I need to satisfy my standards.</u>

Positive affirmation that addresses or negates this fear:

<u>I have a wealth of skills and talent that is waiting to be tapped.</u>

Exercise: Calling your fears by name

Use this exercise to name your fears and formulate reassuring affirmations that can help you address these fears when they crop up.

Fear:

_____

_____

Why I am afraid of this:

_____

_____

_____

_____

How could I overcome this fear or deal with it, should the need arise?

_____

_____

_____

_____

Positive affirmation that addresses or negates this fear:

_____

_____

_____

Fear:

_____

_____

Why I am afraid of this:

_____

_____

_____

_____

How could I overcome this fear or deal with it, should the need arise?

_____

_____

_____

_____

Positive affirmation that addresses or negates this fear:

_____

_____

_____

Fear:

_____

_____

Why I am afraid of this:

_____

_____

_____

_____

How could I overcome this fear or deal with it, should the need arise?

_____

_____

_____

_____

Positive affirmation that addresses or negates this fear:

_____

_____

_____

_____

CHAPTER 11

Eighth Principle of Unconventional Wisdom

Don't Quit While You're Ahead

"Quit while you're still ahead" is probably very good advice for gamblers, who can easily lose all their gains with the next unlucky throw of the dice or turn of the wheel. But life is rarely like a game of roulette, in which winnings come instantly and by pure luck, and losses are sudden, unpredictable, and total. If anything, life is more like a board game in which we move our markers slowly around the course, and make a few gains here, lose a few advances there. Even if we are forced to return to "Go," until the game is finally and irrevocably finished, there is always a chance of catching up. In a board game, you would never quit while you were ahead. You wouldn't even quit if you were behind. There is always the chance that you might win after all, and the only way to find out is to keep playing, and to play hard.

"Don't quit while you're ahead" is my advice to you, once you are well on your way to the life you want to lead. It is so easy to become spooked as you try to change your life. A little failure, an unkind or discouraging word, an unbearable moment of anxiety, or a small mishap can stop you in your tracks. It is quite common for late bloomers to momentarily halt in their advance toward the future, and even to retreat into old ways of being for a few days, weeks, or even months. But if you remember this advice, you will be able to pull yourself out of your quagmires of fear, anxiety, habit, procrastination, or inertia sooner rather than later, and get on with the game.

Two steps forward, one step back is actually a common trajectory for late bloomers. Inevitably, you will heed an old danger signal when it rings inside your head (and seems to reverberate throughout the world around you), and rush back to what looks like safety. This is especially likely when you are just beginning to experience success, because you may not trust it. The new kind of success may feel so unfamiliar that you hardly recognize it as success. Or it may feel so good, and so taboo, that you are sure it will be taken away from you. Perhaps you will feel that you got lucky enough to be successful once, but can't imagine that such rewards can be sustained.

Whatever the reasons, you may find yourself turning your back on success midway through your transformation and rush back to the life you led before. You may try to pick up the pieces, perform mouth-to-mouth resuscitation upon the identities you have laid to rest, and shoehorn your new, expanded self back into the roles you had given up for good. But once you do, the illusory comforts your old life seemed to offer will close in upon you like a trap, and you will realize that you cannot go back without placing all that you have come to value at risk. These are invaluable learning experiences—as long as you extricate yourself quickly. It's quite all right to take a few steps backwards along the way forward—just don't *quit* while you're ahead! The following example from the life of a late bloomer illustrates the virtues of this course.

By all accounts, Ellen was a successful engineer. She had worked in both academic and professional environments, earning high accolades and excellent salaries along the way. At first, she enjoyed the challenges within each of these institutional environments. But as the initial excitement wore off, she began to feel the weight of each bureaucracy bearing down upon her. Within the academic environment, she found that the pressure to continually publish new research and to navigate the tricky shoals of departmental politics diminished her pleasure in the teaching she was hired to do. Within the culture of the consulting firm for which she worked, the constant need to deploy managerial skills to keep projects running smoothly, and the demand to juggle more projects than she felt comfortable handling at once led to a constant sense of anxiety. Ultimately this anxiety materialized in the form of a temporarily crippling work-related disorder—a pinched nerve in her shoulder that made it extremely painful for her to sit and work at a desk for more than ten minutes at a time.

Forced to take a leave of absence for more than a year, Ellen began to rethink her career. She considered changing course completely, abandoning the field in which she had invested fifteen years of her life. But finally she realized that by working as an independent consultant and part-time instructor, she could enjoy all the work aspects she liked, without having to endure the secondary demands that caused so much discomfort. As she began to heal from her disability, she started teaching again on a part-time basis and took on small consulting assignments.

Ellen found that she enjoyed this new balance of work, which allowed her flexibility, less stress, and more time for relaxing hobbies like cooking and hiking. And she found that her disability, though still not entirely healed, was no longer exacerbated by work environments that fostered high anxiety levels . . . until she began to experience a new wave of anxiety. This time, the anxiety was triggered by the lack of predictability that is characteristic of freelancing. Her fear that she would not be able to bring in enough work led her to seek more predictable, salaried employment once again. When a salaried job that seemed to promise security materialized, Ellen accepted it. Yet, as soon as she started the job, she realized she had made a mistake. The managerial nightmares began immediately, and Ellen realized that once again she was going to be asked to handle more projects than she felt comfortable with.

"I realized that I could stay in this job for another year or two and be miserable," Ellen recounted, "or I could quit right away and cut my losses." Ellen weighed the costs of staying, which she knew from past experience were very high, with the costs of leaving and recommitting to her previous work as a part-time teacher and independent consultant. She also considered the many rewards of her brief freelance period, including the flexible schedule and the option of working out of her own home, and soon decided that the better course of action was to quit right away, even if it was a little embarrassing. "I realized that I had successfully attracted clients during my first period of independent consulting without too much effort," she continued. "So why not just operate on the assumption that I could continue to find clients, if I really set my mind to it?"

Experiences like these are tests that put your new convictions through their paces. Like Ellen, if you give up the new rewards that you have fought so hard to gain, you will learn to protect them all the more diligently in the future. By listening to the voices inside your head that send you back, you can gain greater insight into the false alarms that must be recognized for what they are. By trying unsuccessfully to fit back into a skin you have outgrown, you can discover once and for all that there is no turning back for you. And this realization can actually provide a new surge of energy and conviction that will help you to stay in the game and strive all the harder to achieve the life you want to live.

Like Ellen, you may feel embarrassed about reversing ill-thought decisions in order to get back on track. You may feel really silly when you announce to your new boss that you already want to quit. You may experience a bit of chagrin when you tell your family that you have changed your mind about something you seemed quite sure about the month before. Maybe you will worry that your friends and loved ones will think that you are being erratic or indecisive. But who cares what other people think? This is your life, and only you can live it. Sometimes trial and error really is the only way you can learn things about yourself, your work, and your life. It is the course of valor, wisdom, and success to admit a mistake quickly and act on that admission, instead of persisting in a situation that you know is wrong for you.

EXERCISES

Exercise: Getting back on track

The exercise in the previous chapter was designed to help you stop backtracking behavior before it starts. But if you find, like many late bloomers do, that you have retreated into an old and uncomfortable mode of being, this two-part exercise can help you to begin traveling forward again.

Part I: Identifying the pros and cons

1. Take a piece of paper and write across the top the word *Backtracking* (see the example and worksheet provided). In a short paragraph, under this heading, describe the situation toward which you have backtracked or are tempted to backtrack to. This may be a job, a relationship, or an old habit that threatens your well-being.

2. Then create two columns beneath this description. At the top of one column, write *pros,* and at the top of the other, write *cons.* Fill in each appropriate column with all the *pros* (rewards) and *cons* (sacrifices) involved in backtracking to that situation or state. Don't edit yourself too much—just see what comes out.

3. At the bottom of the sheet, or on a second piece of paper, write *Staying on course,* and briefly describe the situation you would maintain, or quickly regain, by once more actively pursuing your vision for the future. This is not necessarily your ultimate destination, just where you would find yourself if you got back or stayed on course.

4. Then create your *pros* and *cons* columns and identify all the rewards and costs that would be involved in committing yourself to staying on course.

EXAMPLE

Exercise: Getting back on track

If you find that you have retreated to an old and uncomfortable mode of being, use this exercise to begin traveling forward again (see additional instructions on previous pages).

Part I: Identifying the pros and cons

Backtracking

Describe the situation toward which you have backtracked or are tempted by, then list the *pros* (rewards) and *cons* (sacrifices) involved in remaining in that situation:

Instead of spending time painting in my studio and trying to learn about the business of art, I keep going to my real estate job. In fact, I am spending more time selling real estate than ever before, even though my heart isn't in it. I thought doing some extra sales work would make me feel less nervous, but it's actually only making things worse because I feel guilty that I'm not in my studio, and I can't really focus all that well on my real estate work.

Pros	Cons
I'm making more money than I would if I were painting.	I'm not giving painting a chance.
It feels more comfortable and less challenging to go to my regular job; I know what I'm doing there.	I feel guilty that I'm not spending more time in my studio; I need to be learning and building a new career.
I feel a little bit more secure about where the money is coming from.	I have that sinking feeling I get when I know I am cheating myself out of something; I am selling myself short.

Staying on course

Describe the situation you could maintain or quickly regain, by staying or getting back on course and once more actively pursuing your vision for the future. Identify the *pros* and *cons* involved in recommitting yourself to your vision.

I need to stick to my original plan of working about 30 hours a week selling real estate and spending 20 hours a week working on my painting career. I need to finish setting up my studio and start painting and planning for a private show of my work.

Pros	Cons
I will be putting in the work I need to actually launch my art career.	I will probably feel uncomfortable, like a beginner, and also, afraid that I might not be able to succeed.
I will truly enjoy the work I do as a painter from a place deep inside of me.	I may feel some growing pains, some fear of letting go of my old identity.
I will be investing in my dreams.	I will have less money temporarily.

WORKSHEET

Exercise: Getting back on track

If you find that you have retreated to an old and uncomfortable mode of being, use this exercise to begin traveling forward again (see additional instructions on previous pages).

Part I: Identifying the pros and cons

Backtracking

Describe the situation toward which you have backtracked or are tempted by, then list the *pros* (rewards) and *cons* (sacrifices) involved in remaining in that situation:

_____

_____

_____

_____

_____

_____

_____

Pros	Cons

Staying on course

Describe the situation you could maintain or quickly regain, by staying or getting back on course and once more actively pursuing your vision for the future. Identify the *pros* and *cons* involved in recommitting yourself to your vision.

_____

_____

_____

_____

_____

_____

_____

_____

_____

Pros	Cons
_____	_____
_____	_____
_____	_____
_____	_____
_____	_____
_____	_____
_____	_____
_____	_____
_____	_____
_____	_____
_____	_____
_____	_____

Part II: Addressing your fears and taking action

1. When you are done writing these lists, ask yourself why you have retreated or are tempted to retreat to an old way of being and jot down your answers (see the worksheet provided). What are you afraid of? What voices are you listening to? Make a list of the fears or assumptions that are holding you back.

2. Are these the same fears and assumptions that you listed in the previous chapter? If so, reread the affirmations you wrote in response to these fears or false assumptions and renew your faith in your ability to transform your life. If not, write some new affirmations that address these fears or negate these false assumptions that threaten to pull you off course.

3. Now, having identified and addressed your fears, reread the two lists of pros and cons that you created in part 1 of this exercise. Ask yourself whether the pros and cons associated with staying on course are more compelling than those associated with backtracking. If so, are you willing to do whatever it takes to stay, or get back, on track? Is it worth experiencing a small amount of embarrassment or making some sacrifices in order to get moving again toward the true rewards you want in your life? If so, make a list of the steps you need to take to get back on track. How soon are you willing to take them? If you can set a date in the near future, then do so and write down this appointment with yourself in indelible ink.

If after completing this exercise you find that you are still reluctant to take action, you may need to spend a little time backtracking. Consider this a search and rescue mission. Perhaps you left some part of your identity behind as you surged forward. You may need to learn more about this part of yourself, the life you have chosen to leave behind, or the calling that is welling up inside of you—by staying right where you are. You need to be patient with yourself and compassionate while this process takes place. Just keep your eyes open to your true values and don't forget the destination you have envisioned while you take this detour. Soon you will feel the strength of your convictions, the energy of your passions, and the voice of your calling pulling you forward once more in the pursuit of happiness.

EXAMPLE

Part II: Addressing your fears and taking action

Review your answers from the first part of this exercise and spend some time thinking about why you have retreated or are tempted to retreat to an old way of being. Then write down some answers to these questions (see additional instructions on the previous pages).

What are you afraid of? What voices are you listening to? What are they saying? Make a list of the fears and assumptions that are holding you back:

I am afraid of jeopardizing my future as a real estate agent. I am afraid of my boss's displeasure when she actually sees me spending less time in the office, even though we've already discussed this. I'm afraid I won't be able to succeed as an artist. I am afraid people will think I'm crazy to give up a respectable career for something as vague as becoming an artist.

I'm listening to a voice that says the world is cruel—that I can only make a living doing something I hate and that there is no chance of surviving if I do something I really love to do. I'm listening to a voice that says I shouldn't take any new risks—that I might fail, and that failure will be a terrible, final thing. I am listening to a voice that says what other people think is more important than what I feel.

Write down some affirmations that address these fears and assumptions:

My career in real estate will be there if I need to go back to it.

If I have succeeded in something difficult before, why not have faith that I can succeed in something new?

The world is generous enough to allow me to do something I love to do and to prosper at it.

Failure is only temporary—if I fall, I can get up again.

What other people think about my career change doesn't matter!

175

What steps do I need to take to get back on track, or stay on track?

1. Start keeping track of how many hours I spend each week on real estate work and stick to my limit of 30 hours/week.

2. Schedule dates in my calendar with myself to spend time in the studio and be there—no matter what (and don't take the phone in there with me).

3. Finish the painting on my easel and start a new one.

4. Find a location where I can host my one-person show, and reserve it.

When can I start taking these steps?
Tomorrow!

WORKSHEET

Part II: Addressing your fears and taking action

Review your answers from the first part of this exercise and spend some time thinking about why you have retreated or are tempted to retreat to an old way of being. Then write down some answers to these questions (see additional instructions on the previous pages).

What are you afraid of? What voices are you listening to? What are they saying? Make a list of fears and assumptions that are holding you back:

_____

_____

_____

_____

_____

_____

_____

_____

_____

_____

_____

_____

Write down some affirmations that address these fears and assumptions:

_____

_____

_____

_____

_____

_____

_____

What steps do I need to take to get back on track, or stay on track?

_____

_____

_____

_____

_____

_____

_____

_____

_____

_____

_____

_____

When can I start taking these steps?

_____

CHAPTER 12

Ninth Principle of Unconventional Wisdom

Push Your Luck

"Don't push your luck" is another one of those gambling proverbs that have made their way into common parlance. While it may not be wise for gamblers to push their luck, considering that good luck is often the only slim reed upon which their success is based, late bloomers can sometimes do well to trust in their good fortune. Like many late bloomers, you may have had too little faith in the generosity of the world. Perhaps you have postponed the pursuit of your dream because you simply didn't believe that it was viable. You may have listened to the negative voices that told you to stop dreaming and start growing up. You may have stopped watching for, and believing in, the signs that say "fairy tales can come true, it can happen to you," as the song "Young at Heart" reminds us. Perhaps you can actually look back and point to the times in your life when you turned a deaf ear or a blind eye to chances offering direct access to your dreams.

If this sounds familiar, then you need to stop and ask yourself where your dreams came from in the first place. If you are honest, you will have to admit that your dreams, along with any talents you have, are gifts—complex, demanding gifts. Life would be a cruel hoax indeed should these gifts come without possibility of pleasurable expression. And yet you may have acted for years on the conviction that the world offers little or no opportunity to fulfill your dreams or follow your bliss.

If you are committed to making your dreams come true, you need to start pushing your luck right now. This means that you need to keep your eyes open at all times, watching for the opportunities that will unexpectedly cross your path. You need to make a conscious decision to live in the land of more, not less. You must shut your ears to the voices that warn you to be cautious, to be moderate in your desires, or to compromise your ideals. Instead, you must pay heed to all the examples of abundance in the world—be they role models who succeed in the walks of life you desire, gestures of kindness and encouragement from people around you, or the simple gifts of each day.

The example of Jonathan, a man transformed from a private, reclusive artist into a financially successful and recognized painter, demonstrates the value of this path. Although Jonathan was encouraged to paint as a child, when he indicated an interest in pursuing an art career as an adult, he was discouraged. His parents were willing and able to pay for Jonathan's college costs, but they refused to cover art school tuition. Instead, they encouraged him to seek a broader education and set his sights upon a more "practical" profession. After a year at a liberal arts school with no degree program in the visual arts, Jonathan dropped out of school and traveled to New York City, where he lived on a shoestring and pursued his passion for painting.

Moved by their son's determination, Jonathan's parents finally agreed to pay for him to attend art school. Having overcome one significant hurdle—gaining his parents' financial support—Jonathan then encountered new hurdles at school. Prevailing teaching trends favored conceptual art over the traditional ideals of beauty and basic tools and techniques of painting that Jonathan was interested in learning. After switching schools, and even disciplines, Jonathan finally left art school and returned to live in New York, where he still hoped to become a successful artist. Again he encountered rejection when he discovered that the art he was interested in making was out of step with popular trends. At that point, Jonathan gave in to the many messages he had received which told him he could never support himself or "succeed" in his artwork. He found ways to support himself by doing odd jobs while he painted in seclusion, rarely showing his artwork except to a close circle of friends. "Although I didn't completely give up the idea that I could succeed as an artist," Jonathan recalls, "I definitely pulled up my bridges for a while."

After several years, Jonathan decided to try a new strategy. He completed a course in commercial illustration and marketed himself to various publications in this capacity. "Suddenly, I found clients who appreciated the fact that I could paint recognizable scenes, and imbue them with beauty and emotion," Jonathan remembers. He quickly won awards and began to attract lucrative assignments from prestigious publications, including commissions to create portraits of actors, musicians, and other newsmakers. "It was wonderful to be paid for my work, to have people see my work, and to feel like I was participating in some kind of dialogue with the marketplace," Jonathan said. The rewards of this situation helped to offset the previous years of rejection and negation. Yet Jonathan still experienced a persistent desire to work as a fine artist, rather than a commercial artist, even though all his previous experience implied that this was an impractical, if not impossible, course.

That was when Jonathan found an opportunity to push his luck, and seized it. Not many years into his career as a commercial artist, Jonathan met a man who was so impressed with his skill at painting likenesses that he asked him to paint a true portrait. "I had always had a certain curiosity about painting fine-art portraits," he recounts. "And here was my chance to try it out." Jonathan accepted the commission and worked hard to create a challenging portrait with not one, but nine, likenesses, which delighted the man who commissioned it. Seeing this occasion as an opportunity to launch a new career more in line with his interest in fine art, Jonathan created several more portraits on a speculative basis and began to promote himself as a portrait artist, using the marketing skills he had gained as a commercial illustrator. Within a few years, he discovered that his biggest problem was no longer dealing with a world that said no to his creative talent, but managing the demands of a world that said yes so often that he was practically painting around the clock.

Jonathan could have easily settled for less in his life, following the career path of least resistance and sticking with it. But, instead, he held on to his dreams, and when fortune placed an opportunity in his way, he jumped at it. In the pursuit of happiness, I encourage you to avoid the temptation to play it safe when new opportunities come along. I invite you to pay heed to those wild dreams which urge you forward. While it may not be advisable to jump at every break or follow every hunch that comes along, you should adopt an attitude of openness and a willingness to consider all the chances that life has to offer, as

Jonathan did, and be willing to push your luck when the opportunity arises.

This principle is not as impractical as it may sound. A common tool that business consultants employ when developing strategic plans is something called "SWOT analysis." SWOT stands for strengths, weaknesses, opportunities, and threats, and a SWOT analysis considers not only an organization's internal strengths and weaknesses, but also the external opportunities to which an organization should be prepared to respond. Strategic planners know that opportunity, when recognized and acted upon, is a vital ingredient to success. With this in mind, they scan the present and immediate future for fortuitous circumstances that can be capitalized upon.

You can take a clue from strategic planners by heightening your own awareness of and receptivity to opportunities that have the potential to hasten or expand the realization of your vision of success. You can put yourself in the path of success, surround yourself with people who are doing well in the way that you hope to, look for opportunities to surge ahead whenever possible, and, whenever bright ideas dawn about new ways to pursue your vision more effectively, create your own opportunities for growth and fulfillment. By being flexible, open, creative, and downright audacious, you may find that life has more to offer than you ever dreamed.

EXERCISES

Meditation: Outward bound

Use this meditation to increase your attitude of openness to unexpected opportunities. When real-life opportunities present themselves, you can employ the exercises that follow to analyze them and decide how best to respond.

1. Begin this meditation by identifying your favorite setting for pleasurable adventure and leisure activities. What environment most pleases and stimulates you, inviting you to explore and enjoy it? Is it a hilly woodland where you can walk, hike, or bike through paths that lead you deep into its mysteries? Is it a gentle stream or rushing river through which you paddle a canoe or navigate a raft, aligning your energies with the powerful currents of the water? Perhaps it is the ocean, and your pleasure comes from swimming or surfing or sailing through its swells. Or maybe your favorite setting is not a natural one at all, but a highly civilized and sophisticated one, like a foreign city you have never visited before or one that you love to visit, year after year. Conjure up this setting now, and place yourself within it, ready to enjoy several hours of pleasant adventure.

2. Imagine that you begin your adventure in a familiar way, starting off your hike on a trail you have traveled before, putting in your canoe at a favorite spot, getting off a train or airplane, or whatever else suits your fancy. Allow the adventure to unfold before your mind's eye as you surrender completely to the pleasure of this excursion. Allow yourself to imagine all the familiar rewards that this adventure promises.

3. Now, open your mind's eye even further—not just to the known pleasures, but also to the unexpected ones. Is there a way that this familiar adventure could be transformed into something even more thrilling and delightful? Do you see a diverging path in front of you that you have never allowed yourself to notice before? If you are on a body of water, is there a new course you can take, or could this be a great opportunity to tie up your vessel and dive deep beneath the water, or simply float along and admire the

sky? Look for the opportunity to transform this familiar journey into an open-ended adventure, and then take it.

4. Allow yourself to imagine the new delights that unfold as you push your luck, heading out into a realm of unfamiliar pleasures and unanticipated experience. Imagine the intense attention you can give to new sensations as you head into the unknown. Perhaps you feel a slight tingling of excitement as you leave the familiar course, the intense pull of desire to explore something new. Or maybe cautious voices urge you to turn back, suggesting that you might get lost, or be late, or have a bad experience. Imagine that you replace any fears or anxieties with the conviction that the world is full of good intentions, gifts beyond your wildest dreams, and rewards for the adventurous. Imagine taking this new direction, and flesh out your vision with earthly and even unearthly pleasures. See it, feel it, taste it, smell it, hear it, and revel in it.

5. Remain with your meditation as long as you like, experiencing the full bounty of the world's gifts. When you are ready, prepare to return to your present life. You can always call up this paradise of possibility by choosing to trust in the good fortune of the universe, to push your luck, and to settle for more, not less. Give yourself the pleasure of this meditation whenever you like, but be especially sure to do so when you feel the walls of your own fears, or the negative messages you receive, closing in on you, narrowing your vision, and hindering your pursuit of happiness.

Exercise: How can I push my luck?

Just like strategic planners, you, too, can stay on the lookout for new opportunities. You can do this by paying attention to what others are doing to get ahead in the areas that interest you and by checking in with your own inner voices to see which new, and possibly unexpected, directions they may be urging you to take. You can also simply make a commitment to staying open to suggestion and being receptive to new ideas or opportunities that cross your path. This exercise will help you to stay alert, creative, and responsive to opportunities to push your luck. The example and worksheet provided offer you step-by-step guides to complete this exercise.

Looking for opportunities

1. Can you think of any people whose lives conform to the vision you have created for yourself? Who has what you want? Who lives the way you want to live? Don't just pick people you know personally. Constantly scan the media for information about others who are living the way you would like to. What can you learn from these people? What daring steps and flying leaps have they taken? How have they pushed their luck? List the actions these people have taken or attitudes they have adopted in order to achieve the kind of success you would like to have.

2. Take some time to think creatively about your future. This is one of those times when you should definitely NOT listen to the Chorus of No. Engage the Chorus of Yes, instead, as you spend ten or fifteen minutes thinking about creative steps you might take to fulfill and even far exceed the dreams you have for your future. Make a list of audacious things you might do or fearless attitudes you might adopt in order to push your luck.

3. Look at these two lists and ask yourself, quite seriously, how you might go about doing any one or more of these things. Which look like actions or attitudes you could take

on right now? How could you do this? Write a few concrete ways in which you might take such an action or
adopt such an attitude in the near future. Also, write a few
thoughts about what might happen if you did. What is the
best possible effect that might result if you pushed your
luck?

Exercise: How can I push my luck?

Use this exercise to open up your life to new possibilities and to respond wisely to those that present themselves.

Looking for opportunities

1. List some people who live life the way you want to and describe actions they have taken or attitudes they have adopted that contribute to their success.

Name:

   Janie S.

Actions/attitudes:

   opened her own gallery and sells her own work to local collectors; has a web site and advertises in magazines to national collectors

Name:

   Bob C.

Actions/attitudes:

   quit work at the real estate company to start his own cabinet-making business; used real estate connections to identify new homeowners and approach them as clients for his new business

Name:

   Martha Stewart

Actions/attitudes:

   combined her interest in the home with good business skills to create a hugely successful multimedia business.

2. Write down a few audacious actions you might take or fearless attitudes you might adopt in order to promote your vision and push your luck:

Create a gallery featuring my work that specializes in "portraits" of people's homes, both interiors and exteriors.

Use my real estate research skills and tools to identify potential clients who are selling old homes or buying new ones and may want a "portrait" of their home. Think big and don't just limit myself to people I know; have faith that there is a national audience for my skills and interests and use a range of media to reach it.

3. How can you translate these actions or attitudes into specific strategies? Describe some concrete actions you can take soon and imagine the exciting results:

Strategy:

Rent a ground-floor retail space for one month and hold a show of my "home portraits." Market the exhibit to a mailing list culled from real estate sources of people selling homes and new homeowners.

Results:

The show might prove so successful that I could open a year-round gallery selling my "home portraits." Then I could create a web site and national advertising campaign that would allow me to reach a national audience. I could have a national sales force marketing my paintings and become a wealthy, full-time painter!

Exercise: How can I push my luck?

Use this exercise to open up your life to new possibilities and to respond wisely to those that present themselves.

Looking for opportunities

1. List some people who live life the way you want to and describe actions they have taken or attitudes they have adopted that contribute to their success.

Name:

_____

Actions/attitudes:

_____

_____

_____

Name:

_____

Actions/attitudes:

_____

_____

_____

Name:

_____

Actions/attitudes:

_____

_____

_____

2. Write down a few audacious actions you might take or fearless attitudes you might adopt in order to promote your vision and push your luck:

_____
_____
_____
_____
_____
_____
_____

3. How can you translate these actions or attitudes into specific strategies? Describe some concrete actions you can take soon and imagine the exciting results.

Strategy:

_____
_____
_____
_____
_____
_____
_____

Results:

_____
_____
_____
_____
_____
_____

CHAPTER 13

Tenth Principle of Unconventional Wisdom

Just Say "Yes!"

Late bloomers have a tendency to say "No!" all too often. They deny themselves their dreams, their desires, their gifts, and the bounty of the universe. Behind all this denial lies fear—fear of change, of failure, of rejection, of death, and even of life, with all its capricious ways. Every single late bloomer's story that I have heard boils down to a tale of fear. There are late bloomers who are so terrified that they will be rejected by their family, their friends, or by society at large if they pursue their dreams that they stay locked in frustrating lives. There are late bloomers who are so afraid to challenge old thoughts and habitual behaviors that they repeat the same frustrating patterns over and over again rather than risk an encounter with the unknown. There are late bloomers who are so sure that each new day is full of threats and dangers that they box themselves into safe and suffocating lives that offer the illusion of security.

Although you cannot completely avoid your fears while you go about changing your life, you can at least make an effort to minimize them and prevent them from ruling you anymore. You may not be able to silence your anxieties, but you can learn how to say "Shhh!" to them every so often. You may not be able to forget the past experiences that first taught you to say "No!" to yourself so often, but you can decide to stop dwelling upon them for a change. The tool that can help you do this is the word "Yes!" and all of the healing and empowering acceptance that it conveys.

I invite you to say "Yes!" not only to tomorrow, but also to yesterday, and today. Say "Yes!" to your dreams, "Yes!" to your callings, "Yes!" to your persistent hankerings, and "Yes!" to your opportunities. Accept your unhappy memories as reminders of the past, not rulers of the present, and resuscitate your happy ones as harbingers of the future. Say "Yes!" to that part of you that needs permission to say "No!" to others from time to time. Put yourself first for a change, and leave your doubts behind. Plug into the power of positive thinking. Pronounce your positive affirmations out loud. Place yourself smack in the middle of the world of "Yes!" and act as if you believe these words of the American poet E. E. Cummings:

> *yes is a world*
> *& in this world of*
> *yes live*
> *(skilfully curled)*
> *all worlds*

Begin your journey of life change with an attitude of accept- .
ance by saying "Yes!" to your past, acknowledging and accepting
immutable truths about who you are, and why. This may mean
deciding to express aspects of your personality that you have tried
to suppress over the years because you thought they somehow
rendered you unworthy, flawed, strange, or ineffective. Why
work against nature? If you are dreamy, ambitious, curious,
obsessed, talented, eccentric, driven, introverted, or highly extro-
verted, by accepting and celebrating these aspects of your character, you may find that they will bear fruit in ways you can't even
imagine. If some damaging experience (like repeated humiliation
in school) or some vulnerable aspect of your nature (like intense
sensitivity) has held you back over the years, simply accept it as
part of the game. Like a handicap in a race, it may slow you down,
but it won't take you out of the running. You need to stop fight-
ing these things and begin working with them instead. Perhaps
you can even find ways to transform your perceived flaws and
your painful experiences into assets.

The next way to saying "Yes!" is by accepting and celebrating
the present. Late bloomers have a tendency to postpone happiness. You may be so accustomed to feeling frustrated about
your life, your work, or your relationships that you live entirely
for the future, when you hope things will get better, rather than
in the present, when the real potential for change exists. Do
you realize that the moment you allow yourself to articulate
your vision for the future, you actually begin living within the
reality of that vision? There is no reason why you should postpone happiness until you attain your final goal. You can begin
by looking for the gifts that come each day in which you honor
that vision, whether they are the surge of energy you feel when
you apply yourself to a new challenge, the triumph you experience when you refuse to submit to external expectations or old

standards of judgment, or the pleasure you find in a reward that you have worked very hard to earn.

By being fully—and positively—in the present, you can grow more aware of the opportunities to pursue your vision that come each day and quickly act upon them. You can also become more aware of the temptations and discomforts that threaten to pull you off course. You can give yourself permission to say "No!" when it is appropriate (and hear the "Yes!" you say to yourself and your dreams when you do so). You can also grow more conscious of the challenges and obstacles you encounter each day and begin the process of overcoming them or working around them before they have a chance to overwhelm you.

Finally, I invite you to say "Yes!" to the future you want, embracing it as an inevitable reality rather than a far-off dream. Shout down the naysayers, both inside your head and out, who tell you the world is too small and your dream is too big. Remind yourself that this is your life, and you have permission to live it however you like. Once you do, you will enter the world of "Yes!" where your dreams await expression. The story of Jerri, a late-blooming writer and poetry therapist, illustrates that power that affirmative thinking and acting has to transform lives.

Jerri's journey as a writer began early. She started writing poetry at the age of eight, and imagined that she would follow in her father's footsteps when she was an adult by writing for the newspaper he edited. But subtle and overt forms of negation made themselves heard early on in her life. "I had a lot of low-self-esteem issues," Jerri recalls. "I received many messages that who I was, inside and out, was not okay." When she announced her intentions to work for her father's paper, her desires were thwarted. "My father said he wouldn't hire me because people at the paper would either be too easy on me or too hard on me," Jerri recalls. "I realize now that he was trying to protect me, but at the time, I was devastated."

Determined to find a way to write for a living, Jerri began working in the field of public relations and advertising. The reputation she gained as a hard worker, and an effective one, bolstered her sense of self-esteem for nearly fifteen years. But the pressure of her work was intense, and the feeling that she was betraying her real self began to weigh down upon her over the years. "Often I was in situations where I didn't feel confident or comfortable. The world I was in felt fake. I knew I was not being true to myself," Jerri explains. After refusing to listen to these feelings for a period of years, Jerri began to experience alarming episodes of disorientation. Twice she lost her way as she drove to work and couldn't remember where she was going. Then she felt the entire left side of her face and her left arm go numb. "My therapist suggested that I was virtually scared stiff, I was so afraid of losing myself," Jerri remembers.

After this last episode, Jerri finally accepted the fact that the work she was doing was dangerously undermining her sense of self, and she gave herself permission to quit. At the time, she was in a new marriage that offered her economic freedom, and she decided to accept that gift, too. She also decided to honor her long-ignored calling to write creatively by signing up for a playwriting workshop. The play she wrote was ultimately produced and Jerri continued writing, working her way back to her first love, poetry. For Jerri, saying "Yes!" to her calling didn't mean getting published, or even making money at it. It just meant allowing herself to be authentic. "It took me many years to get back to who I always knew I really was," she recounts. "When I started writing full-time, I began to reclaim that person I had been all along."

While Jerri continued to nurture her authentic self, she also became more watchful for opportunities to express that self creatively in her daily life. This increased awareness helped her to find a creative way to connect her love of poetry with her desire to help others struggling with painful emotional issues. "I stumbled across a very small blurb about the National Association for Poetry Therapy (NAPT) in a magazine I was reading, and I called for information," she recalls. She enrolled in the association's training program, which included many hours of fieldwork, and began working as a poetry therapist. Some of her earliest work was with teenage girls with low self-esteem. Within two years of contacting NAPT, Jerri received their annual award for outstanding achievement in the field. Even though publication was not one of her goals, she even found herself writing a column about poetry therapy in a local newspaper.

As Jerri progressed in her journey of saying "Yes!" to herself and the opportunities around her, she even learned to find the "Yes!" that is buried inside of rejection. Before becoming a poetry therapist, Jerri had applied to a highly competitive graduate program for poetry and had been turned down. Although she felt terrible about this rejection at first, Jerri says, "I now wonder, 'What would I do with a master's degree in creative writing?' I am so much more effective and fulfilled as a poetry therapist. To what I considered a setback at the time, I now say, 'Thank you.' Whenever you are being rejected," she adds, "I believe you are being protected."

Jerri's advice to other late bloomers reflects her approach to reclaiming and translating her calling into work, a philosophy that is both proactive and practical. "Find and hold onto the courage to be who you are, no matter who that is. Be reasonable and logical about how you go about doing this. You have to be practical and find out how to support the essence of who you are," she says. "Find the way within the career that works for you."

Like Jerri, you can cultivate attitudes of acceptance about

your calling and positiveness about the world in which you pursue it. By doing so, you can forge a creative and authentic path through the landscape of your life. Instead of listening to the negative voices that tell you to sacrifice your dreams and give up because the challenges are too severe, you can search for the path of "Yes!" and wind through, over, and around the obstacles that would otherwise block your passage. A conscious commitment to positive thinking allows you to become more sure-footed, more creative, and more determined as you pursue your dreams, and you can translate your vision of the future into immediate reality by recognizing the opportunities and the gifts that are scattered along your way.

The following meditation provides you with an opportunity to discover the power of "Yes!" that lies inside you. The writing exercise that follows it offers you a chance to travel deep inside yourself and find the beliefs or fears which may be blocking your way. By learning more about these beliefs or fears, and articulating a positive affirmation that negates them, you can begin to chip away at that mental block and cut a path for the power of "Yes!" to break through, once and for all.

Keep in mind the fact that your fears are not completely unfounded. More likely than not, they were shaped by painful, all too real experiences. But this does not mean that the negative messages you have taken from these experiences are true. Scientists have learned the hard way that what looks like reliable evidence can often support erroneous conclusions. Instead of defining your life by the negative experiences that reinforce your old fears or beliefs, you must seek out new experiences that will support the beliefs by which you wish to live.

EXERCISES

Meditation: Water around stone

So many images from the natural world illustrate the powerful inclination of things to find their way. When water in a stream encounters an obstacle in the form of an immovable rock, the water shifts, flowing around and over the rock, and rushes and cascades along on its course. If a log blocks its path, the water streams over it until eventually it dislodges the log and carries it downstream, or it simply breaks it down into bits and pieces. In some cases, water will actually change the landscape through which it flows, carving a new riverbed where there was none before. Think about the Grand Canyon, for instance. The will of water is so strong that people have long harnessed it to generate power, with old-fashioned waterwheels and modern hydroelectric plants.

Have you ever watched a time-lapse film that captures the journey of a new plant growing from a bulb or root? A soft yet insistent green shoot forces soil out of its way, twists around pebbles and stones, and pushes toward the sun's light and heat. It is amazing that something so tender can be so strong. Welsh poet Dylan Thomas wrote a poem celebrating the phenomenon of this power, writing "the force that through the green fuse drives the flower drives me." In the fairy tale about Jack and the beanstalk, the upward thrust of a huge plant enables a relatively weak young boy to approach and ultimately overcome a large and evil giant.

I invite you to recognize your own life force—the energy inside of you that urges you on, and that has the power to overwhelm obstacles, the flexibility to bend and twist, and the unstoppable will to keep flowing and growing.

1. Take a few moments to sit with your eyes closed and connect with that power inside you. Feel the restless stirrings of your heart and mind, your desire to transcend, your will to live, your drive to succeed, your lust for life. Then, try to translate this power into an image—a tangible force with which you are familiar, whether it takes the form of a flower, a river, a gust of wind, a light in the darkness, or any other image that comes to mind.

2. Once you have selected an image that conveys the power inside you, imagine this force at work in the world. Allow yourself to travel with it as it moves over and around obstacles, shifts course, and finds its way. Follow it in your mind's eye, and even allow yourself to be carried along with it. Albert Einstein used to imagine traveling alongside a light beam, rushing through the universe at the speed of light. By practicing this meditation, he penetrated many secrets of the physical world.

3. Remember that this force lies inside you. Whenever you feel discouraged, blocked, or frustrated, conjure up this image and recall the sense of power that it conveys. Recognize the vital energy that is surging inside you. Remember that it is there, and harness its power whenever you need it.

Exercise: Affirming your truth

In chapters 10 and 11, you developed a series of positive affirmations to respond to old fears and anxieties that threatened to trip you up. With this exercise, I invite you to travel deep within yourself and find the single fear or negative belief that most threatens your sense of well-being and that most frequently crops up to block your way. Once this fear has been identified, you will find that you are much better prepared to say "No!" to it and "Yes!" to your life by repeating a life-affirming response. Follow the directions below and record your thoughts using the format suggested on the worksheet at the end of this chapter.

1. Reread the fears that you wrote down in the exercises "Calling your fears by name" (chapter 10) and "Addressing your fears and taking action" (chapter 11). When you have done this, ask yourself whether there is a single fear or belief that connects or undergirds all these fears. What idea most frequently comes between you and the expression of your vision? What one thought has the power to stop you in your tracks or send you scurrying back for shelter and safety? Write down your answer and keep refining it and boiling it down until you come to a single negative idea that is the source of all your other fears.

   For me, this idea was the belief that I would be punished or abandoned for expressing my authentic self. I believed that I would be loved, rewarded, and cared for only as long as I defined myself in terms of others' needs, instead of in terms of my own. I was afraid that defining myself and my life in terms of my own needs and impulses would surely lead to emotional, social, and financial disaster. No wonder it took me decades to discover that I could make a living, earn respect, and gain personal pleasure by honestly expressing myself in my life and work. This new belief became the positive affirmation that fueled my life change.

2. Once you have identified your most threatening belief or fear, try to formulate a positive affirmation that contradicts this message and suggests an alternative way of being and believing. Play with the ideas and words that come to you

until you arrive at a message that best communicates a belief that can support you in your pursuit of happiness and fulfillment. When you are done, write it down.

3. Study this phrase for a while and try to believe it with your whole heart and mind. Can you feel this message strengthening your creative power and multiplying your natural resources? Are you prepared to live as if you believe this positive affirmation is true? If so, then get ready to say "Yes!" to this belief in every part of your life.

You have a choice to make every day—and several times within each day: You can live as if you believe that your worst fears are true, or you can live in the faith that what you most hope for yourself and for the world is true. If you live according to your new affirmations, evidence will soon prove beyond a shadow of a doubt that your faith is justified. Just say "Yes!" to what you most want to believe, and you will hear that "Yes!" resounding throughout the world. Live as though your vision for the best of all possible lives is at hand, here and now, just waiting for you to reach for it. Remember, you are living in a world of infinite potential. Fulfill it!

EXAMPLE

Exercise: Affirming your truth

Use this exercise to identify the single fear or negative belief that most frequently crops up to block your way, and respond to it with an empowering and reassuring affirmation.

1. With one sentence, describe the single negative idea or fear that is the source of all your other fears.

Fear:

No one will like me unless I sacrifice my own needs in order to meet other people's needs.

_____

_____

2. With one sentence, create a positive affirmation that contradicts the above idea or fear by suggesting an alternative way of being and believing.

Affirmation:

I can make myself happy by putting my own needs first, and may even please other people in the process.

_____

_____

Exercise: Affirming your truth

Use this exercise to identify the single fear or negative belief that most frequently crops up to block your way, and respond to it with an empowering and reassuring affirmation.

1. With one sentence, describe the single negative idea or fear that is the source of all your other fears.

Fear:

_____

_____

_____

_____

2. With one sentence, create a positive affirmation that contradicts the above idea or fear by suggesting an alternative way of being and believing.

Affirmation:

_____

_____

_____

_____

PART THREE

Planning and Pursuing Life Change

Late bloomers have been known to fulfill their potential without the help of a formal, written plan of action. Sometimes this blossoming comes about because the late bloomer experiences a sudden epiphany that lights his or her way—a breakthrough that releases the person from the past and catapults him or her into the future. Successful personal and professional transformations can also be jump-started by lucky breaks that suddenly clear the path for callings that have long been repressed or blocked by insurmountable obstacles. Yet like most late bloomers, you have probably grown weary of waiting for that sudden focusing of vision or drive, that earth-shattering epiphany, or series of highly fortuitous, catalyzing events. Or perhaps you are actually fortunate enough to have experienced a moment of clarifying inspiration, yet you still find yourself holding back, unsure of the way to translate this experience into a more satisfying life.

The central purpose of the Ten Principles of Unconventional Wisdom is to prime you for change: to help you break through mental and spiritual blocks, to invite you to question the well-meaning but often misguided advice that has hampered you in the past, and to direct you toward new sources of faith, hope, courage, and momentum that will energize you now and in the future. They are designed not only to clear your inner roadways, but also to make you more aware of the opportunities and possibilities that await you in your external life. By reading and adopting these principles, you have oriented yourself for change. By practicing the steps provided in the following chapters, you can translate your readiness into a plan of action that will direct you through your transformation.

In the following pages, you will find some tried-and-true planning techniques that professional consultants use to help organizations create strategic plans. I have adapted these techniques to meet your needs as a late bloomer. By working through these exercises, you can write your own strategic plan that combines common sense with unconventional wisdom to create a powerful program for change.

You do not need to wait any longer to transform your life. By combining emotional, intellectual, and spiritual readiness with pragmatic planning techniques, you can actually plan your transformation now, and begin following your plan immediately. I invite you to take a few days or evenings to read the following chapters and complete the exercises in them. Then you will have at the ready a personalized travel plan that will guide you toward the destiny you desire, as soon as you wish to start.

CHAPTER 14

What's stopping me from getting started?

Identifying the Challenges

You have probably spent many delicious hours daydreaming about that elusive time far off in the future when you will actually be leading the life you want to live. These are the dreams that keep hope alive as you struggle through a day-to-day existence that feels increasingly frustrating, boring, or alienating. Yet when you start listing the many challenges that lie between you and your dreamed-of destination, fear and hopelessness probably descend. These challenges may grow in your imagination, looming larger and larger, until they assume the solidity of insurmountable obstacles, completely blocking the path between you and the future you desire. As any list-maker knows, however, as soon as you sit down to translate the multidimensional universe inside your head to the simple two-dimensional surface of a sheet of paper, the tasks seem to shrink back down to size.

List-making is the beginning of purposeful action. It allows you to name, quantify, and prioritize activities that otherwise threaten to overwhelm you. As a list-maker myself, I am aware of the sense of calm and purpose that list-making can induce. Yet there is a flip side to this process. Lists can also be frightening. Recently, when I had far too many balls in the air at one time, I thought making a list would reassure me that the obligations and challenges I faced were achievable and surmountable. Instead, once I completed my three-page list of things to do, I could only respond by simultaneously laughing and crying. The list actually *was* unachievable, at least in the time frame I had set for myself. Once I stopped to count how many balls I was juggling, I realized I couldn't possibly continue to keep so many of them in the air, and they started falling spontaneously from the sky. "I should never have stopped to count," exclaimed one part of my brain. Yet another, wiser voice chimed in, saying, "Now that you *know* you've got too many balls in the air, you can *decide* which ones to drop."

This example points out the two virtues of list-making. First, it helps in translating the unnamed and unquantified challenges that lie ahead into concise, measurable, achievable tasks. And secondly, by so doing, list-making provides the opportunity for realistic problem-solving and strategizing. It allows you to move from the cloudy realm of anxiety to clearheaded realism and pragmatism. If there is too much to do in the allotted time, you can cross off some items and place them on another list of things to do—later. Or you can extend the amount of time you have scheduled in which to accomplish the tasks. And you can go back over the items that remain on the list and number them in order of priority and achievability. Finally, you can actually begin taking the actions listed and cross them off, one by one, creating a reassuring record of your progress.

From my own personal experience as a late bloomer, as well as my observation of other late bloomers, I have realized that the challenges we deal with fall into two distinct categories: the tangible, and the intangible. Tangible challenges include things like "saving enough money to take six months off from paid employment," or "getting into graduate school." Clearly these are real challenges that will require significant amounts of effort, discipline, and sacrifice to overcome. Yet the intangible challenges, like "overcoming the social taboos associated with giving up my job as a lawyer," or "bolstering my self-esteem to the point where I can stop worrying about pleasing others and work on pleasing myself," often prove to be the most obstinate blocks to our progress.

The biggest mistake I have seen myself and other late bloomers make is to jump into the tangible challenges without first resolving, or at least recognizing, the intangible ones. I cannot tell you how many times I have seen late bloomers (including myself) make courageous false starts toward visions of fulfillment and happiness—quitting jobs, setting out on adventures, attempting new kinds of work—only to find that unresolved intangible conflicts swamp their boats and send them paddling back to shore. For this reason, you must consider *all* the challenges—material, emotional, and spiritual—before you begin to plan for life change. The following meditation and writing exercise will help you to identify and describe a comprehensive list of the challenges which you will encounter in your path toward your new future.

PLANNING EXERCISES

Exercise: Listing the challenges

In several of the previous meditations and exercises, you envisioned the challenges you will need to overcome in order to reach your desired destination. In this two-part planning exercise, I invite you to write your challenges down in as thorough a list as possible. This exercise includes a list-making activity designed to help you identify your most obvious challenges, both tangible and intangible, as well as a meditation that will help unveil hidden challenges. When you have completed this exercise, you will have listed the major challenges that must be addressed by your plan of action. Keep in mind that this is not the time to worry about *how* you are going to address these challenges. That will come in the following chapters. It is simply an opportunity to list your challenges as thoroughly as possible.

1. Make a list of the challenges you need to meet in order to move from your present state to the vision you have described for yourself, considering all the categories listed below (see the example and worksheet provided). If some of the categories don't apply to your situation, then skip them. Feel free to add other categories that do apply.

   Work Experience

   Education/Vocational Training

   Money

   Time

   Relationships

Physical Resources (equipment, real estate, furniture)

Emotional/Spiritual Issues

For example, you might write "need to get more massage therapy training" under Education/Vocational Training, or "I've got to stop putting other people's needs before my own" beneath Emotional/Spiritual Issues. If you need more time to devote to your calling, you might write "find a way to get two days off each week to pursue my new interests" under the Time heading. If your partner isn't respecting your needs or supporting your goals, then under Relationships, you might write "Figure out how to deal with my unsupportive partner." If you can't get any work done because of distractions from family members, young and old, you might write under Physical Resources, "need to get a room of my own—with its own door, lock, and key."

2. Reread the list you have just written. As if you are watching a movie about your life, actually envision yourself taking each action as you travel from your present life to the one you desire. Don't just tick off the ideas as if you are proceeding through a mental list—actually *visualize* yourself working through them. Pay attention to the emotions you experience as you imagine dealing with these challenges: the exhilaration and the excitement, as well as the anxiety and fears. Make some notes on your list regarding the anxieties or fears that come up for you along the way. These may provide clues to intangible challenges that you will need to overcome. Do not leave these challenging issues off your list! These are the intangibles that can pull you right off course or block your future progress.

3. Under the appropriate headings on your list, add in the new challenges you have become aware of that reflect

215

these fears and anxieties. For example, if you found your-self worrying about what your mother would say when you announced that you were quitting your job, you might write, "stop worrying about what my mother is going to think," under Relationships. If a little (or big) voice kept saying, "What makes you think you can do this?" when you listed the challenges you would need to meet in order to pursue your calling as a career, you might add "find a way to deal with low self-esteem" under Emotional/Spiri-tual Issues. If you recognized a tendency to avoid certain tasks as you identified challenges that have tripped you up in the past, you might jot down "figure out how to stop procrastinating" under Time.

4. Once you have completed your list of tangible and intangi-ble challenges, number them, starting with the challenge that is most pressing—the problem that must be solved, or the action that must be taken before you can proceed. Keep numbering the challenges until you have organized them into a logical sequence that reflects the order in which you will need to deal with them, from start to finish. If some of the challenges are directly related, you can give them the same number (see the example provided).

Exercise and Meditation: Listing the challenges

List the challenges you need to address in order to achieve your vision. When you are done, number them in the order they need to be handled.

Work Experience

(#8) I need to improve my painting skills.

(#9) I need to learn how to market my paintings.

(#12) I need to learn what's involved in running my own gallery.

Education/Vocational Training

(#8) I may need to take some classes in order to acquire the level of painting skills I want.

Money

(#3) I need to cover my basic living expenses while I make the transition from being a full-time realtor to becoming a full-time artist.

(#5) I need to get some start-up funds to pay for setting up my studio, painting supplies, and occasional rental of exhibition space.

(#13) Ultimately, I need to make enough money from my painting to allow me to give up my real estate work.

Time

   (#4) I need to free up 10–20 hours a week to start painting seriously.

Relationships

   (#2) I need to figure out how to stop putting my boss's needs first.

   (#1) I need to stop worrying so much about what other people are going to think about me and my work and figure out how to satisfy myself.

Physical Resources

   (#6) I need a studio where I can shut the door and ignore the phone.

   (#7) I need a new easel and some painting supplies.

   (#10) I need a home computer to organize my mailing lists and design invitations and price lists.

   (#11) I need a place where I can exhibit my artwork.

Emotional/Spiritual Issues

   (#1) I need to have enough faith in myself and my calling to start working in earnest as an artist.

   (#2) I need to not surrender to my people-pleasing instincts.

Exercise and Meditation: Listing the challenges

List the challenges you need to address in order to achieve your vision. When you are done, number them in the order they need to be handled.

Work Experience

_____
_____
_____
_____
_____
_____
_____

Education/Vocational Training

_____
_____
_____
_____
_____
_____
_____

Money

_____
_____
_____
_____
_____
_____
_____
_____

Time

_____

_____

_____

_____

_____

_____

Relationships

_____

_____

_____

_____

_____

_____

Physical Resources

_____

_____

_____

_____

_____

_____

Emotional/Spiritual Issues

_____

_____

_____

_____

_____

_____

CHAPTER 15

How do I get from here to there?

Writing a Travel Plan

If you are really serious about reaching the destination you desire within the foreseeable future, you must plan your transformation like you would a road trip, plotting a detailed itinerary that will guide you through the rough and lonely spots you may encounter along the way. If you set out without a plan in place, you are likely to wander off the track, take time-consuming detours, or go around in circles. Or you may try an overly ambitious route that dooms you to failure. But if you plan your strategies ahead of time, you can consciously use all the wisdom you have accumulated to trick yourself into succeeding, capitalize upon your hidden strengths, and avoid triggering your fear mechanisms when you encounter challenges that have the power to throw you off track.

For example, before I had a clear plan for launching my career as a writer, I had a tendency to make abrupt changes that undermined my ultimate vision. Whenever I became overwhelmed by the feeling that I was doing the wrong thing with my life, I would quit my day job even though I had no next move in place. The fear of financial instability that followed these resignations would then drive me back to the nearest paying job I could find—*before* I had had sufficient time to launch a successful writing career. I wasted a lot of time repeating these mistakes until I developed a plan that took the urgency of my calling *and* the power of my fears into consideration.

This plan described a series of steps that made it possible for me to support myself through part-time work while I laid the foundation for a financially successful career as a writer. With its gradual series of goals and tasks, each building upon the last, this plan helped me to move purposefully toward my vision. It reminded me to be patient when I was eager for change, and to remain calm even when my whole professional and personal identity was in transition. It helped me to stay on track and to follow a practical path toward a vision that had, for many years, seemed as remote and mythical as the lost island of Atlantis.

The process you need to follow in order to create your plan is very similar to that used by organizations that are planning change. Strategic planners create a vision statement fairly early on in the process, describing where the organization needs to be in a few years. Then they do something called "gap analysis," measuring and defining the "gap" that lies between where the organization is now and its desired future condition. Once planners define the challenges that must be met, they develop strategies to handle these challenges creatively and effectively.

These strategies usually take the form of sequential goals and supporting tasks. The goals describe major accomplishments that address the challenges identified. The tasks refer to the smaller steps that are required to accomplish these goals.

Does some of this sound familiar? In previous exercises, you have described your vision for the future and identified the challenges that must be met in order to bridge the gap between your present condition and that future which you desire. The following exercises will help you to translate this information into a sequence of goals and tasks that will guide you through your journey. Like professional strategic planners, you will begin by writing a rough draft of your goals and tasks, which you can refine later on in the process.

Your goals will describe how you plan to address the challenges identified in the previous exercise. Once you have outlined these goals, you will find it fairly easy to draft a task list detailing the specific actions that will help you to accomplish your goals. While goals usually refer to major accomplishments that can take as long as six months to a year or more to complete, tasks will describe actions that you can accomplish in a few days, weeks, or, at the very most, several months. Your tasks should include activities that require little more than your own investment of time, energy, and money, as well as those that depend in part upon the cooperation of the outside world.

As a rule, you should build in backup plans to accompany goals and tasks that are largely dependent upon outside factors. Sometimes the world takes longer to cooperate than you would like, or a particular goal may require several efforts and various strategies before it can be successfully achieved. For example, an artist might have a goal of traveling to France to study the work of the French Impressionists. His first task might be to apply for a grant from a foundation to underwrite his trip. Since there is no guarantee about winning such a grant, the artist might include a backup plan to finance his trip by working as a part-time graphic artist. Should all his plans go awry, he could still study the works of French Impressionists included in local museum collections and illustrated art history books.

Some of you may resist describing your future journey in such detail. Maybe you are the kind of person who likes to think on your feet, or prefers to trust in fate. Or perhaps you are hesitant to lock yourself into a rigid path when the world is so full of risk, change, and unexpected opportunities. As a late bloomer, a strategic planner, and a seasoned traveler, I can assure you that it is better to have a good plan and be willing to change it than to go forward with no plan at all. When you begin taking the actions that will change your life, you are likely to experience spells of intense anxiety and doubt, resistance (both internal and external), procrastination, and indecision . . . even desperation. Having a plan in hand that reminds you of the next step you need to take, as well as your long-term goals, is essential to guide you through these periods.

This does not mean that you cannot adjust your plan along the way to respond to the unexpected opportunities or pitfalls you will encounter. Keep in mind that organizations rarely follow their strategic plans to the letter. Some goals end up taking much longer to achieve than expected, while others seem irrelevant once the time comes to implement them. Plan your future the way you would like it to unfold, then revise your plan as needed to account for unexpected events, new information, and changes of heart and mind.

As you start to draft your plan, you may find that you really don't know how to go about meeting certain challenges. When strategic planners encounter this difficulty, they go straight to the experts for advice. You can do the same thing. If you know people who have successfully addressed challenges you must deal with, get their advice. Ask these experts to tell you how they did it, what they did right, and what they would do differently if they had another chance. Then judge for yourself what approach makes the most sense to you. You might also get some good ideas from books or information available on the Internet, should your challenge be one that is widely shared, like breaking into a specific field, or coping with an addiction or emotional pattern. Once you have done your research, you will find it much easier to define your goals and describe the tasks needed to achieve them.

When you write your rough plan for change, don't forget to incorporate the Ten Principles of Unconventional Wisdom. Think about when you should bite off more than you can chew in order to get ahead. Try to imagine the point at which you will be able to leap into your new life, regardless of whether you have resolved all your fears and anxieties. Anticipate when you will be ready to put all your eggs in one basket—and dedicate all your resources to the achievement of your vision. And remember to build in a little pleasure along the way. Plan some goals or tasks that promise immediate, delightful gratification. After all, the purpose of all this planning is not to *hurry* you toward a finite state of happiness. It is to guide you gradually through the active pursuit of happiness, a pursuit which will begin as soon as you depart from your dead end of demonstrated dissatisfaction and start moving toward your heart's desire.

EXERCISES

Exercise: Listing goals and tasks

In this exercise, you will create a rough draft of the goals and tasks that will form the framework of your plan for change. Use the following exercise to describe the most effective ways you can imagine to meet the challenges that separate you from the destination you desire. You will have a chance to refine these goals and tasks in the following chapter, so don't get too hung up on the details now. Before you start, you might want to take a look at the sample plans provided at the end of this chapter, which include good examples of goals and supporting tasks. Worksheets and an example are also provided to help guide you through this process.

1. In the last chapter, you listed the tangible and intangible challenges that lie between you and the fulfillment of your vision for the future. Create a new list now by writing those challenges down again in the order you gave them in the previous exercise.

2. Starting with your top challenge, think about the best way you can address that challenge, and write this solution below the challenge. Achieving this solution will be your goal. Begin each goal with a verb that describes the action that you should take. A few examples follow:

Challenge: Need to get more massage therapy training.
    Goal: Complete a massage therapy training and licensing program.

Challenge: I've got to stop putting other people's needs before my own.
    Goal: Create a support network that will help me to remember to put my own needs and desires before others'.

Challenge: Find a way to get two days off each week to pursue my new interests.
    Goal: Exchange my full-time job for freelance consulting work that pays a higher hourly wage and permits me greater scheduling flexibility.

Challenge: Need to get a room of my own—with its own door, lock, and key.

Goal: Remodel the guest bedroom as my home office.

3. When you have finished listing your goals, return to the top of your list and describe a series of tasks beneath each goal. Remember, tasks are actions that take only a few days, weeks, or, at most, months, to complete. If you find that you are stumped when you try to describe your tasks, this could be a good opportunity to consult some experts. This is also the point at which you can build in backup plans for goals and tasks that may prove particularly challenging, as demonstrated in the example below from my own plan for change.

Goal: Support myself completely from my writing (e.g., put all my eggs in one basket).

Tasks: 1. Write a book proposal that matches my talents and interests with current publishing trends.

2. Submit this proposal to an agent who can help find a good publisher and negotiate a favorable advance.

3. Find a publish who is willing to pay an advance that will cover one year of my living expenses.

4. Quit my part-time job and begin writing full-time.

5. If I can't sell the book, hold on to my part-time job until income from my writing covers all of my living expenses.

6. Revise my book proposal, or develop a new one and repeat tasks 1–3.

7. Try to get high-paying article assignments from national magazines while I wait for a satisfactory book contract.

4. When you are done, reread the goals and tasks you have listed and ask the following questions:

Have I really started at the beginning? Is the first goal something that I can begin working on right away?

If not, add in a goal and some tasks at the beginning of your list. You want to be sure that your plan starts with actions you can begin taking immediately.

Are there gaps in my plan? Have I forgotten to address some challenges that might trip me up?

If so, fill in the gaps with extra goals, tasks, or backup plans. Remember, the purpose of your plan is to lead you gradually through all the challenges you can envision in order to prevent you from running into brick walls or falling into potholes along the way. Try to describe a smooth, gradual transition without any major gaps.

Do my goals and tasks take me all the way to the destination I desire?

If not, make sure that you add more goals or tasks to get you to the end of your list. You want this plan to carry you all the way through your transition, not to leave you high and dry, halfway there. You may even want to add a final set of goals and tasks which describe what you will do once you get to your desired destination, whether this is to celebrate in some way or even to begin planning a new journey.

Exercise: Listing goals and tasks

Using the format below, follow the instructions provided on the previous pages to create a rough draft of your plan for life change.

Challenge

__I need to have enough faith in myself and my calling to start working in earnest as an artist.__

Goal

__Put myself and my calling as an artist first in my life__

Tasks

__(1) begin each day with a period of prayer and meditation during which I focus my attention and spiritual resources on answering my calling as an artist__

__(2) take at least one action every day that translates my calling into reality__

Challenge

__I need to figure out how to stop putting my boss's needs first and to stop surrendering to my people-pleasing instincts.__

Goal

__Stop putting other people's needs (including my boss's) first__

Tasks

__(1) spend some time in therapy focusing on these issues__

__(2) start setting boundaries with my boss; when she makes unrealistic demands, let her know that I can't meet them__

__(3) put aside time each day that is entirely focused on my needs and interests__

__(4) use my calendar to schedule things that matter to me and don't reschedule them unless absolutely necessary__

Challenge

I need to cover my basic living expenses while I make the transition from being a full-time realtor to becoming a full-time artist.

Goal

Go part-time with my real estate job until I can afford to quit it

Tasks

(1) figure out exactly how much money I need each month

(2) talk to my husband about ways we can cut back on our living expenses

(3) figure out how many hours I will need to work selling real estate to meet my reduced needs (talk to other part-time realtors to get a good idea of what's involved in working part-time and what I can expect to earn)

(4) talk to my boss about going part-time with my real estate job

(5) sell real estate part-time until income from my painting sales equals, and eventually surpasses, income from real estate sales

Challenge

I need to free up time to start painting seriously.

Goal

Free up 10–20 hours/week by cutting back paid employment and housework

Tasks

(1) get my husband and kids to do some extra household chores so I can paint on evenings and weekends

(2) go part-time with my job and use that time plus free time on evenings and weekends to paint

Exercise: Listing goals and tasks

Using the format below, follow the instructions provided on the previous pages to create a rough draft of your plan for life change.

Challenge

_____

_____

Goal

_____

_____

Tasks

_____

_____

_____

_____

_____

_____

_____

Challenge

_____

_____

Goal

_____

_____

Tasks

_____

_____

_____

_____

_____

_____

Challenge

_____

Goal

_____

Tasks

_____
_____
_____
_____
_____
_____
_____

Challenge

_____

Goal

_____

Tasks

_____
_____
_____
_____
_____
_____
_____

SAMPLE PLAN

Peter, late-blooming personal chef

Vision

I will give up my more-than-full-time work as a lawyer to become a part-time personal chef, preparing healthy and delicious meals for regular clients who will savor and appreciate my work. I will enjoy learning more about food and cooking on an ongoing basis and sharing that knowledge with others. I will live a balanced and nurturing life that integrates work with activities like spending time with my family, reading, traveling, and doing volunteer work. I will earn less than I did as a lawyer, but I will have more balance, find more pleasure in my work, and have time to enjoy a well-rounded life. Income from well-managed investments, combined with lower living expenses, will help to offset the decrease in my earnings.

Goals & Tasks

Make time to explore my interest in cooking

   Cut back legal practice to four days a week

Explore different cooking experiences

   Cook lunches for my wife's friends as if I were catering on
      my days off
   Work in the kitchen of my friend's restaurant
   Begin organizing and maintaining a recipe file

Research cooking schools

Obtain catalogues from schools

Visit schools I'm interested in

Compare schools regarding tuition, length of program, location (and cost of living there), average age and size of class, work opportunities offered while in school, etc.

Apply to schools

Figure out how to finance my education and professional transition

Prepare a current and future budget in order to figure out what expenses I will have to cut out (e.g., second car) and which I will maintain (e.g., travel)

Compare cities my wife and I would like to move to regarding quality and cost of living

Calculate how much income could be derived by selling our house, combined with income from savings and investments, to cushion the transition period

Determine how much my wife and I will have to earn through part-time work in order to produce enough income to keep us from dipping into our savings

Learn more about how to invest money, particularly in mutual funds

Go to cooking school and start earning income as a personal chef

Sell house (*note*: This ended up taking far longer than Peter anticipated; he continued to practice law part-time and polish his cooking skills in various ways while waiting for the sale.)

Give up legal practice

Relocate to Boston to attend cooking school

Complete cooking school

Find part-time work in food-related activities, like working in a retail gourmet store

Begin working as a private chef for hire while completing my degree

Keep expanding the variety of recipes in my file

Launch professional career as personal chef

Move to new city with higher *quality* of living and lower *cost* of living

Advertise for clients

Work as a personal chef 3–4 days a week

Continue learning about food and expanding my recipe file

Create a lifestyle that minimizes stress and allows me and my wife to participate in a variety of activities that we enjoy

Keep my new work part-time

Make sure that my work environment is positive and that I am fairly compensated for my work

Never let work sap my energies in a destructive way and adversely affect my life again

Keep work just one aspect of a life filled with other interesting and fulfilling activities: time with my wife, family, and friends; reading history books; traveling; attending movies and performing arts shows; eating out; volunteering for causes that engage me; etc.

SAMPLE PLAN

Lily, late-blooming freelance writer

Vision

I will quit my job at the advertising agency to work as a full-time freelance writer, writing articles—and eventually books—on subjects that fascinate me. I will dedicate my time to this new work, which uses my best talents, gives me pleasure, and provides pleasure to my readers. I will stop doing work that saps my energy, makes me unhappy, and is of dubious value to the world at large. I will work approximately eight hours a day, five days a week. I will have plenty of free time to exercise and pursue other interests. I will stop putting other people and their needs first in my life, and devote my time to my own needs and interests.

Goals & Tasks

Quit my job at the advertising agency

Calculate how much I can reduce my living expenses by getting a roommate, cutting out unnecessary luxuries, etc.
Determine how much of my investments I am willing to cash in, and how long they will cover my living expenses (*note:* Lily found that cashing in a quarter of her investments allowed her to go six months without paying work.)
Get up the nerve to quit by remembering that this is MY life and I need to stop wasting it
Enlist the support of my friends to help me do this

Prove to myself that I am serious as a writer

Set up an inexpensive home office with everything I need to be a professional writer (computer, good-quality printer, desk, light, reference books)

Read some books about writing and selling magazine articles and follow the advice in them (*note:* Lily decided that this course was preferable to attending graduate school, which she ultimately felt would take too long, without offering any real advantages.)

Attend trade conferences and seminars for writers

Subscribe to trade magazines for writers

Devote a significant amount of time (4–6 hours) to writing on weekdays, whether or not I am getting paid

Write every day, whether I feel like it or not

Deal with the emotional fallout I might experience

Schedule regular lunches and coffee breaks with friends and mentors who support me

Look for role models whom I can get to know and emulate

Start keeping a journal to serve as an outlet for my anxiety as well as a progress report

Try to exercise regularly, meditate, and keep up spiritual practices

Continue to see my therapist until my anxiety level becomes manageable

Start writing articles and pitching them to magazines

Research magazines that publish articles on subjects that interest me

Write a few sample articles and start sending them to editors
Write query letters to editors telling them about my general
  interests and soliciting assignments to write in these areas
Call editors and try to engage them on the telephone

Get published and get paid

Get some examples of my work published by writing articles
  for free or low-paying magazines or community newspapers, which are all easy to approach
Use these examples to show off my skills to more upscale
  publications
Start getting paying article assignments, ideally 1–2 major
  articles a month
If it takes longer than six months to start getting regular
  magazine assignments, get a part-time job that is not
  demanding and neither drains my energy nor engages my
  people-pleasing tendencies

Write a book proposal and find a publisher

Develop a proposal describing the book I want to write
Submit book proposal to a number of agents and select an
  agent who can make the best deal for my book
If I don't find an agent or a publisher for this book within a
  year, try a proposal on a different subject that might be
  more popular

Balance magazine and book projects with other interests for a wonderful life

Write the above-mentioned book
Keep writing magazine articles

Start earning higher pay as a writer

Begin making public appearances as a writer (lectures, conferences, etc.)

Keep a balance of other activities in my spare time (gardening, home improvements, time with family and friends, etc.)

CHAPTER 16

Is there a better way?

Creating Strategies That Work

A good plan for change is much more than a simple list of things to do. At its best and most effective, a life plan is a highly creative strategy that approaches challenges from a variety of perspectives. For this reason, strategic plans for organizations are rarely written by a single individual. They are created by planning committees whose members bring a variety of perspectives to the process. Sometimes each member of the committee develops his or her own individual recommendations about the best way to address the challenges that are in question, and presents these strategies for discussion by the group at large. Sometimes the group as a whole conducts brainstorming sessions during which the members throw out various ideas for consideration until a strategy which incorporates a range of suggestions is agreed upon.

Inevitably, committees include several different personality types. There is usually the conservative who says, "This is the way it has always been done; that is how we should do it." Then there is the radical or free spirit who says, "I have this crazy idea, but it just might work." There is the pessimist who points out all the dangers and past failures, who urges the highest degree of caution, and advises against risk. And there is the optimist, the person who believes that greater success is always possible, and who is in favor of trying new ideas and boldly traveling to new heights. Finally, there is the pragmatist who evaluates each suggestion calmly and reasonably, balancing risk against gain, strength against weakness, the familiar against the unknown. The pragmatist helps the committee combine the most efficient, appropriate strategies to get to the desired destination.

Don't these committee members sound familiar to you? How often do you listen to the debates between your internal optimist and pessimist? Haven't you toyed with wild notions of ways you could change your life, only to hear the discouraging voice of that fearful voice which always squashes new ideas in favor of old, familiar ways of doing things? Haven't you also heard that good, sound voice of reason from time to time—that relatively impartial moderator who monitors these internal dialogues and keeps them from getting bogged down or out of control? This is the voice that says, "That's enough from you," when the internal naysayer gets overly shrill and insistent; the voice that shouts, "Bravo!" when the optimist finds a brave new solution to a persistent problem; the voice that inquires, "Why not give that a try?" instead of fearfully shouting down any new idea.

To prepare your plan for life change, you need to hold your own planning committee meetings in which you propose a variety of strategies and select the winning combination of goals and step-by-step tasks. This is creative problem-solving at its best. Although it may sound like a lot of work, it is actually quite engaging and enlightening. If you give each voice inside your head a chance to speak, you can learn a lot about yourself. The exercise in this chapter is designed to help you conduct your own personal planning committee meetings, so you can translate the first draft of your plan into a thoughtful and effective strategy for life change—a strategy that balances moderation and caution with hope, faith, and ambition.

EXERCISES

Exercise: Consulting your planning committee

This planning exercise will give you the opportunity to review your rough draft of goals and tasks from several points of view. By listening to the various voices inside your head, you can consider a variety of ways to achieve your goals, strategies which alternately reflect optimism, innovation, conservatism, and caution. The example and worksheet at the end of this chapter will provide you with a simple format to organize your thoughts. At the close of this exercise, you will settle upon a set of strategies that combines the best of these perspectives.

1. Begin this exercise by getting in touch with your internal optimist—that part of you that believes in happy endings, triumphal marches, and the benevolence of the universe. Reread your list of goals and tasks from the perspective of this optimist and allow yourself to envision them successfully guiding your progress toward your vision. Then ask yourself these questions:

Have I been hopeful enough?

Does my plan reflect the belief that the world will meet me at least halfway if I make an effort to share my gifts, talents, and energies?

Does it reflect a rock-solid faith that the fulfillment of my vision is within reach?

Are there some shortcuts I can take or some leaps of faith that I can build into my plan?

How would I write my plan differently if I were to be truly optimistic about my future and my ability to succeed?

How can I tackle some of the challenges more creatively, more assuredly, or more faithfully?

When you have answered these questions, write down your new ideas. For example, perhaps you made an unconscious decision to leave out that bit about applying to the top school in your field, asking for a loan to start your new business, or getting a hot agent to represent your screenplay, because you thought you were asking too much of yourself and of the world. Now is the time to go back and add in those ambitious, optimistic, and courageous goals and tasks. Don't edit your optimist now. Revise your plan by adding in some new goals and tasks or rewriting old ones (see the example and worksheet).

2. Now, go through this same process engaging the voice of your internal radical, your wild child, your free spirit, or your maverick entrepreneur. This might be a good time to reread the thoughts you wrote down in the exercise "How can I push my luck?" (chapter 12). Then look at the goals and tasks you have identified and ask yourself the following questions:

If I decided to become completely radical and innovative about pursuing my vision, what would I do differently?

Have I been bold enough? Creative enough? Audacious enough?

Have I proposed tasks that are truly challenging?

Have I identified the moments when I will need to bite off more than I can chew, put all my eggs in one basket, and push my luck?

This time, allow yourself to think outside of the box. Consider the people you know who have "made it"—not by trudging along the beaten path, but by bushwhacking through wild terrain . . . rappelling down steep cliffs . . . and spelunking through dark caverns. Are there ways that you can achieve your vision sooner rather than later? Are there actions you can take that might catapult you to success? High-risk, high-reward strategies that just might work? Or is there simply some wild and wacky idea that appeals to your more eccentric side? Revise your plan by adding in some new goals and tasks or rewriting old ones.

3. Finally, ask for the perspectives of your most conservative voice and your inner pessimist. Find out what you are afraid of, what actions drive your discomfort level through the roof, and where you want to tread carefully rather than march briskly toward the future. This is the chance for your Chorus of No to have a word or two. Give the chorus the floor as you ask yourself the following questions:

If I were going to be very, very careful and avoid unnecessary risk or anxiety, what would I do differently?

Have I factored in backup plans and safety nets that will keep me from panicking or giving up if my riskier strategies don't work out as planned, or take longer than I imagined?

Have I built in opportunities to strengthen my confidence, and controls to nip my fears in the bud?

As you answer, allow yourself to imagine the most cautious path you could take toward your vision, building in safety nets and support networks, factoring in additional, more gradual goals and steps, and doing what you can to avoid setting off your alarm systems. There is no reason for you to create a plan that promises to keep you in a perpetual state of discomfort, or one that exposes you needlessly to risk. Sometimes your inner pessimist is trying to protect you. Your inner conservative wants what's best for you, too. Listen to what these voices have to say, and when you are done, revise your goals and tasks once more.

4. Now your committee meeting is almost over. All that remains is for you to narrow down the various strategies you have considered into a preferred course of action. This time, you need to get your whole committee working at once. Assign your most reasonable inner voice to be a moderator. Whenever you feel that one particular voice—whether it is your optimist or your pessimist, your radical or your conservative—is taking over, steer the discussion back to the middle ground. Your plan needs to include strategies that represent a balance of these voices—ones that are optimistic enough to keep you moving forward, radical enough to jolt you out of old ruts, cautious enough to avoid needless risk, and conservative enough to prevent anxiety from overwhelming your progress.

Reread each of the strategies you have developed so far and mark asterisks next to the elements you deem best—the winning ideas that seem to have the best chance of getting you from here to there, the ones that truly excite you, or just look like they will work. If some of the ideas your "committee members" came up with seem too risky, too cautious, or too eccentric, you can leave them out of your plan for now. But be sure to throw in a few fast-and-fancy moves to keep your optimist and free spirit engaged. And don't forget to build in some backup plans to satisfy your inner conservative and pessimist. This whole committee is coming along for the ride. If you don't consult them at the onset of the journey, there is a good chance that they will mutiny before you arrive at your final destination.

5. When you are done, write down your final strategy—your final list of goals and tasks in the order they need to be taken. Make sure that you have included tasks that address the whole of your life—not just work, relationships, and financial interests, but also leisure, spiritual, emotional, and physical well-being, and pure and simple pleasure. And don't throw out your notes. There is always a chance that the strategy you have selected might not work out exactly as you have planned it. You can always fall back on a more conservative, or a more outrageous, strategy if that happens.

When you are satisfied with your plan, you will probably want to share it with someone else. If you decide to do this, be careful about whom you choose to share your strategies with. Most late bloomers have at least one close friend, colleague, mentor, or counselor whose judgment they trust, and who can serve as a sounding board for their plans. Unfortunately, not everyone can react objectively, no matter how hard they may try. Always consider the source when you get feedback—the feedback may reflect more upon the person who is giving it, and his or her own experiences, than upon you and your plans. Ultimately, you, and the committee inside your head, are the right judges of what is best for you.

EXAMPLE

Exercise: Consulting your planning committee

Use this exercise to review your rough draft of goals and tasks from several points of view and revise it into an effective set of strategies.

1. Tune into your most optimistic voice and reread your goals and tasks. Can you think of any more optimistic, faithful ways that you might go about pursuing your vision? If so, rewrite the changed goals and tasks accordingly.

Original Goal

Find an art dealer or gallery owner who wants to represent my paintings for sale

Revised Goal

*Be my own dealer—rent a gallery space periodically and hold exhibits twice a year

Revised Tasks

*1. Hold a summer show at Janie S.'s gallery

*2. Hold a second show near Christmastime, either at the gallery, another space, or at home

*3. If these shows are successful, continue to hold semi-annual exhibitions of my work

Original Goal

Revised Goal

Revised Tasks

_____
_____
_____
_____
_____
_____

2. Tune into your internal radical, your wild child, your free
   spirit, or your maverick entrepreneur, and reread your goals
   and tasks again. Can you think of any more creative, innovative ways that you might go about pursuing your vision?
   If so, rewrite the changed goals and tasks accordingly.

Original Goal

   Market my "home portraits" to clients of the real estate agency
I work for

Revised Goal

   *Develop a comprehensive marketing plan promoting my "home
portraits" to a wide range of local and national buyers

Revised Tasks

   *1. Have a working lunch with my friend Rita J., who is a public
relations and marketing consultant, and get her advice
   *2. See if Rita will accept a painting from me in exchange for
developing a comprehensive public relations and marketing plan
   *3. Pursue my public relations and marketing plan and reach a
large and diverse clientele with my work

_____

Original Goal

_____

Revised Goal

_____

Revised Tasks

_____

249

_____

_____

_____

_____

_____

_____

3. Tune into your inner conservative and your anxious pessimist, and read your goals and tasks once more. Do you need to build in some backup plans and safety nets in order to limit your risk and keep your anxiety level down as you pursue your dreams? If so, rewrite the changed goals and tasks accordingly.

Original Goal

  Quit my real estate job and paint full-time

_____

Revised Goal

  Go part-time with my real estate job until income from painting sales equals or exceeds income from real estate work

Revised Tasks

  1. Talk with my boss about going part-time with my job

  2. Try to work 30 hours/week at real estate sales and 20 hours/week at painting

  3. Actively sell paintings in order to raise income from artwork as quickly as possible

  4. Track income from real estate and painting sales and prepare to quit my job once income from painting becomes sufficient to cover my basic living expenses

Original Goal

_____

Revised Goal

_____

Revised Tasks

_____

_____

_____

_____

_____

_____

4. When you are done, reread your strategies and mark asterisks next to the elements you deem best—the winning ideas
   that seem to have the best chance of getting you from here
   to there, the ones that most excite you or just look like they
   will work.

Exercise: Consulting your planning committee

Use this exercise to review your rough draft of goals and tasks from several points of view and revise it into an effective set of strategies.

1. Tune into your most optimistic voice and reread your goals and tasks. Can you think of any more optimistic, faithful ways that you might go about pursuing your vision? If so, rewrite the changed goals and tasks accordingly

Original Goal

_____

_____

Revised Goal

_____

_____

Revised Tasks

_____

_____

_____

_____

_____

_____

_____

_____

Original Goal

_____

_____

Revised Goal

_____

_____

Revised Tasks

_____

_____
_____
_____
_____
_____
_____

2. Tune into your internal radical, your wild child, your free
   spirit, or your maverick entrepreneur, and reread your goals
   and tasks again. Can you think of any more creative, innovative ways that you might go about pursuing your vision?
   If so, rewrite the changed goals and tasks accordingly.

Original Goal
_____
_____

Revised Goal
_____
_____

Revised Tasks
_____
_____
_____
_____
_____
_____
_____

Original Goal
_____
_____

Revised Goal
_____
_____

Revised Tasks
_____

_____

_____

_____

_____

_____

_____

3. Tune into your inner conservative and your anxious pessimist, and read your goals and tasks once more. Do you
   need to build in some backup plans and safety nets in order
   to limit your risk and keep your anxiety level down as you
   pursue your dreams? If so, rewrite the changed goals and
   tasks accordingly.

Original Goal

_____

_____

Revised Goal

_____

_____

Revised Tasks

_____

_____

_____

_____

_____

_____

_____

Original Goal

_____

_____

Revised Goal

_____

_____

Revised Tasks

_____

_____

_____

_____

_____

_____

4. When you are done, reread your strategies and mark asterisks next to the elements you deem best—the winning ideas
   that seem to have the best chance of getting you from here
   to there, the ones that most excite you or just look like they
   will work.

CHAPTER 17

How do I prepare for the journey?

Making a Resource List

There is nothing more annoying or, in some cases, even frightening, than taking off on a trip and not packing everything you need. In the days before automatic teller machines were located at major intersections in most cities around the world, running out of money could be a real problem for tourists. Not packing enough clothes, or the right clothes, for a trip could lead to physically uncomfortable or socially embarrassing situations. For a backpacking trip, it is essential to pack carefully and thoughtfully. No one wants to carry an overloaded backpack for days on end. But running out of food, or forgetting essential items, is a real danger if a good packing list isn't written down and followed to the letter.

When organizations create strategic plans for their future, planners spend a great deal of time analyzing the resources the organizations will need to achieve their goals. These usually include more time and labor, staff with greater or more specific expertise in certain areas, different equipment, larger offices, more money, and so on. In order to do this, organizations assign one or more people to read through the goals and tasks described and make a list of the specific new resources that will be needed to achieve them. This list serves as the basis for a budget, a new staffing plan, an equipment and facilities plan, and so on.

You can avoid a great deal of anxiety and discomfort by identifying ahead of time the resources you will need to complete your life change. Something as simple as "finding the time" or "coming up with the money" can stump late bloomers for years if these issues are not addressed head-on, and in the beginning. I know a late bloomer who needed $10,000 to launch her new career. She couldn't find any bank willing to give her a small business loan, and she couldn't find any individual to lend her the cash. So she added an extra $10,000 to her mortgage when she refinanced her loan following a home improvements project and deposited the extra money into a savings account to finance her professional transition.

Peter, the late-blooming chef, knew that he needed to take a day off each week from his law career in order to explore his interest in cooking professionally, but he didn't want to lose any income during this exploratory period. When his secretary quit, he decided not to replace her. He took on the extra clerical duties himself, working a few extra hours every evening. The money he saved allowed him to take the day off each week to explore his new career without experiencing a significant dip in his income.

These are just two examples of creative ways late bloomers have solved the two most common resource problems: not enough money and not enough time. What these examples demonstrate is that once you become clear about the resources you need, you are much more likely to find creative ways to gather them. The following exercise will not only help you to create a thorough resource list, but even more important, to build strategies into your plan to make sure you will get these resources when you need them. By planning ahead, you can avoid getting stranded halfway through your journey.

EXERCISES

Exercise: Creating a resource list

1. Start this exercise by taking a blank sheet of paper and creating two columns (see the example and worksheet provided). At the top of the left-hand column, write *Resources* and list the following headings below, leaving several spaces between each one:

   Time

   Money

   Equipment and Facilities

   Education and Experience

   Outside Assistance

   Emotional, Spiritual, or Physical Support

   Leisure and Rewards

2. When you are done, read through your goals and tasks, and whenever you come across an item that will require a resource that you don't currently have, make a note underneath the appropriate heading. For example, if one of your goals is "going to cooking school," then write "cooking school" under Education and Experience. Since this is going to cost money and require an investment of time, note the cost of tuition under the heading Money, and the amount of time it will require under Time. If making that time is going to require some extra hours of childcare, then write that under the heading Outside Assistance, and add the cost of those extra hours of childcare under the heading Money.

If you are not good at estimating costs and hours, then you might want to ask a friend to help you with this process. Some of us are simply better at budgeting than others. If you know you tend to underestimate or overestimate the amount of time or money it takes to do things, then try to compensate for that tendency while you work on your resource list.

The first five headings in this resource list are the needs that most people identify when they set out to make major changes in their lives. Whether they realize it or not, most late bloomers will also require additional physical, emotional, and spiritual resources to complete their transformations (as well as these more prosaic items). Some late bloomers may need to improve their physical condition in order to bring about the changes they want in their lives. Strategies for boosting physical well-being can include quitting smoking or losing weight, treating allergies or other debilitating conditions, increasing time spent exercising, or adding yoga or regular massages into one's routine. Fortunately, opportunities for improving your emotional or spiritual well-being are widespread and readily accessible, ranging from free or inexpensive ones like meditation, self-help programs, support groups, and spiritual practices, to more costly alternatives like therapy, expert-led courses, and retreats. Try to be honest about your needs in these areas and factor them into your resource list.

Also, try to foresee the ways that you may want to reward yourself for all this hard work. Factor in some incentives. Will you need to take more breaks than usual? Can you take a vacation? Is there a hobby or leisure activity you need to remember to build into your schedule? Is there a particular reward that you would like to give yourself for a job well done? Try to include a few of these ideas on your resource list, too.

3. Once you have read through all your goals and tasks and completed the list of resources you will need to get in order to fulfill them, take several moments to review this list. It can be tempting to create an inflated, unattainable resource list in order to justify continued procrastination. Do you really need all these things? Could you do without some of them if you needed to? Are there any ways to kill two birds with one stone? For example, if you need to get experience in a new field and you also need to earn a little extra money, would it be possible to get a paying internship or to find some other way to get paid while you learn? It is equally tempting to create a list that seriously underestimates your real needs. Perhaps you are so eager to get to your destination that you are overlooking real resource needs that must be addressed if they are not to trip you up along the way. It is better to include these on your list, even if they are somewhat intimidating, than to leave them off entirely.

4. Return to your resource list and at the top of the right-hand column, write *Strategies*. For each resource listed on the left-hand side of the page, suggest a strategy describing how you can go about getting this resource in place (see the example provided). Think about the best and most efficient way that you can get the money, the time, the experience, and the support you need to change your life. Be sure to bring both your internal optimist and your free-thinking innovator to this process. This is also a good time to consult people you know who have successfully gathered similar resources. They will have some good strategies to recommend.

If a few of the items on your list completely stump you now, don't worry. Most people find that necessary resources become available to them along the way. Just try to plan ahead as best you can and pack what you will need for your journey. Now, you are almost ready to embark.

EXAMPLE

Exercise: Creating a resource list

List the resources you will need to complete your goals and tasks under the appropriate headings in the left-hand column. In the column on the right, jot down strategies that will help you get these resources in place. Remember to make your strategies as optimistic and creative as the goals and tasks you have enumerated.

Resources   Strategies

Time
1/2 hour each morning for   Ask my husband to take on
prayer and meditation   weekday breakfast preparation
_____   so I can have quiet time; get
_____   whole family to agree that I
_____   can have 1/2 hour quiet time in
_____   the guest room each day
20 hours per week for painting Start with 10 hours per week
_____   by setting aside 5 hours dur-
_____   ing the week and 5 hours on
_____   weekends; go part-time with
_____   my real estate job in order to
_____   work up to 20 hours per week
_____   painting time
_____   _____
_____   _____
_____   _____
_____   _____
_____   _____

Money

Shave $10,000/yr off my annual expenditures in order to make going part-time with my real estate job possible	Give up gym membership and start running; don't buy any new clothes unless essential; eat out less at restaurants; take cheap vacation w/ borrowed mountain cabin instead of expensive vacation this year
Earn $5,000 from painting in first year	Sell 10 paintings at $500 each; sell these at private showings at my house, through real estate connections, and exhibit at Janie S.'s gallery

Equipment and Facilities

Home studio for painting and related activities: meditating, correspondence, etc.	Set up guest room as studio; put bed in attic; set up old easel; buy paint supplies; take desk from living room; set up corner for meditation
Find a gallery space I can use once or twice a year for professional exhibitions	Talk to people with galleries (Janie S., for example) who may want to rent out their spaces when they are out of town, taking vacations, etc. If that doesn't work, find a cooperative gallery that I like; also, use our home as a gallery

Education and Experience

Better painting skills	Practice, practice, practice; take private lessons with a local painter to improve skills and learn new techniques, if necessary
Art marketing skills	Barter painting(s) with Rita J. to develop a marketing plan and get some ideas

Outside Assistance

Marketing consultant	(see above)
Painting teacher	(see above)
Additional therapy	(see below)

Emotional, Spiritual, or Physical Support

Family support

Have a "meeting" with my husband and children; let them know that I will need their support to get this new work going; get them to brainstorm with me; make sure that they are "on board"; find out how I can reward them for their help and sacrifices

Additional therapy

See if my therapist will barter a painting in exchange for some extra sessions to focus on my people-pleasing issues and to help me center myself creatively

Professional support

Find or start a support group of women artists with whom I can share the professional, spiritual, and personal challenges of becoming a self-supporting artist

Leisure and Rewards

Reward myself for my focus and hard work in this new career

In addition to the work itself being a reward, create other rewards like "feasts of the senses"—candlelight dinners with husband, country picnics with family, solo visits to museum shows—to nurture my senses and stimulate my creativity

Family vacations and solo getaways

Be sure to take one family vacation each year, but cut expenses by driving and by borrowing friends' vacation homes; do the same for occasional solo getaways

Exercise: Creating a resource list

List the resources you will need to complete your goals and tasks under the appropriate headings in the left-hand column. In the column on the right, jot down strategies that will help you get these resources in place. Remember to make your strategies as optimistic and creative as the goals and tasks you have enumerated.

Resources   Strategies

Time

_____   _____
_____   _____
_____   _____
_____   _____
_____   _____
_____   _____
_____   _____
_____   _____
_____   _____
_____   _____
_____   _____
_____   _____
_____   _____
_____   _____
_____   _____
_____   _____
_____   _____

Money

_____ _____
_____ _____
_____ _____
_____ _____
_____ _____
_____ _____
_____ _____
_____ _____
_____ _____
_____ _____
_____ _____
_____ _____
_____ _____
_____ _____

Equipment and Facilities

_____ _____
_____ _____
_____ _____
_____ _____
_____ _____
_____ _____
_____ _____
_____ _____
_____ _____
_____ _____
_____ _____
_____ _____
_____ _____
_____ _____

Education and Experience

_____   _____
_____   _____
_____   _____
_____   _____
_____   _____
_____   _____
_____   _____
_____   _____
_____   _____
_____   _____
_____   _____
_____   _____
_____   _____
_____   _____
_____   _____

Outside Assistance

_____   _____
_____   _____
_____   _____
_____   _____
_____   _____
_____   _____
_____   _____
_____   _____
_____   _____
_____   _____
_____   _____
_____   _____
_____   _____
_____   _____
_____   _____

Emotional, Spiritual, or Physical Support

_____   _____
_____   _____
_____   _____
_____   _____
_____   _____
_____   _____
_____   _____
_____   _____
_____   _____
_____   _____
_____   _____
_____   _____
_____   _____
_____   _____

Leisure and Rewards

_____   _____
_____   _____
_____   _____
_____   _____
_____   _____
_____   _____
_____   _____
_____   _____
_____   _____
_____   _____
_____   _____
_____   _____
_____   _____
_____   _____

CHAPTER 18

How do I write my plan?

Putting It All Down on Paper

Congratulations! You have almost finished writing your plan for life change. The rest of the planning process involves nothing more than organizing your ideas in a user-friendly format and plugging in some dates that will remind you to stay on-time and on-track as you change your life. You may wish to write your plan by hand or prefer to use a computerized word-processing program, which will allow you to edit your plan more easily and add new goals or alternative strategies as you progress. Whichever approach you prefer, the instructions provided below, along with an example and worksheet, will direct you through the process of writing your final plan. Once you have completed this exercise, you will be ready to work through the exercises in the following chapter, which will help you to schedule the successful completion of your plan.

EXERCISES

Excercise: Putting it all down on paper

1. Take a blank piece of paper or open a new document screen in a word-processing program and write *Vision* at the top of the page or screen in bold letters (see the example and worksheet provided). Beneath this heading, copy the vision statement you created in chapter 3. If you find that your original vision statement needs to be revised to reflect discoveries you made about yourself and your dreams while working through the exercises and meditations provided in the previous pages, then make these changes now.

2. Underneath your vision statement, write the words *Goals & Tasks* in bold letters on the left-hand side of the page. On the far right-hand side of the page, write the word *Scheduling* in bold letters.

3. Reread the lists of goals and tasks that you have developed in response to the exercises provided in chapter 15: *How do I get from here to there?*, chapter 16: *Is there a better way?*, and chapter 17: *How do I prepare for the journey?* Mark asterisks next to all the best strategies that you developed in these exercises, identifying the goals and tasks that seem to have the greatest likelihood of succeeding. Then write numbers next to them, indicating the order in which they will need to be achieved.

4. Under the heading *Goals & Tasks*, write down your first goal in bold letters. Beneath it, describe in list form the

tasks you will need to complete in order to achieve that goal. Continue to write down all your goals and tasks, using this same format. Be as specific and thorough as possible so that this final plan will guide you, step-by-step, to achieving the vision you have described for yourself.

5. Leave the *Scheduling* column blank until you have completed the exercises in the following chapter.

EXAMPLE

Exercise: Putting it all down on paper

Following the instructions provided on the previous pages, write down your vision statement, goals, and tasks in the order they will need to be achieved using the format below. Leave the scheduling section blank until you complete the exercises in chapter 19.

Vision

I will dedicate my life to my painting. I will make sure that making art plays a role in my everyday life, whether by actually working in my studio, reading about art, thinking about paintings, taking classes, going to galleries and museums, etc. As long as necessary, I will continue to work as a realtor, but I will negotiate a deal with my boss that will allow me more flexible hours to provide regular time for painting. I will learn how to sell my paintings, and work hard until income from painting supports my basic needs and those of my family. Ultimately, I will give up selling real estate for good.

Even though I may be putting in longer hours for less pay for awhile, I will be fueled by the knowledge that I am finally answering my calling. People will begin to recognize my hidden talents; I will stop feeling like an impostor. I will feel a new level of joy and authenticity that will be expressed through my work and my daily life. I will no longer feel the need to "feed" my dissatisfaction by smoking and overeating. I will want to take care of my body so that I have energy to do the work that excites me. I will also make sure to have time for activities like gardening and being with friends and family that nurture and relax me.

Goals & Tasks	Scheduling
Put myself and my calling as an artist first in my life	3/1–ongoing
(1) ask my husband to take on weekday breakfast preparation so I can have quiet time; get whole family to agree that I can have 1/2 hour quiet time in the guest room each day	3/1–ongoing
(2) begin each day with a period of prayer and meditation during which I focus my attention and spiritual resources on answering my calling as an artist	3/1–ongoing
(3) take at least one action every day that translates my calling into reality	3/1–ongoing
Stop putting other people's needs (including my boss's) first	3/1–ongoing
(1) spend some time in therapy focusing on these issues	3/1–2/28
(2) start setting boundaries with my boss; when she makes unrealistic demands, let her know that I can't meet them	3/1–ongoing
(3) put aside time each day that is entirely focused on my needs and interests	3/1–ongoing
(4) use my calendar to schedule things that matter to me and don't reschedule them unless absolutely necessary	3/1–ongoing

Goals & Tasks	Scheduling
Get the outside support I need to make these changes in my life	3/1–6/30
(1) Have a "meeting" with my husband and children; let them know that I will need their support to get this new work going; get them to brainstorm with me; make sure that they are "on board" and find out how I can reward them for their help and sacrifices	3/1–3/31
(2) See if my therapist will barter a painting in exchange for some extra sessions to focus on my people-pleasing issues and to help me center myself creatively	3/1–6/30
(3) Find or start a support group of women artists with whom I can share the professional, spiritual, and personal challenges of becoming a self-supporting artist	3/1–ongoing
Set up the guest room as a painting studio	3/1–3/31
(1) Put the bed in the attic	3/1–3/31
(2) Set up my old easel	3/1–3/31
(3) Buy painting supplies	3/1–3/31
(4) Set up corner for meditation	3/1–3/31

Goals & Tasks	Scheduling
Go part-time with my real estate job until I can afford to quit it	4/1–ongoing
(1) figure out exactly how much money I need each month	4/1–4/30
(2) talk to my husband about ways we can cut back on our living expenses	4/1–4/30
(3) figure out how many hours I will need to work selling real estate to meet my reduced needs (talk to other part-time realtors to get a good idea of what's involved in working part-time and what I can expect to earn)	4/1–4/30
(4) talk to my boss about going part-time with my real estate job	5/1–5/31
(5) sell real estate part-time until income from my painting sales equals, and eventually surpasses, income from real estate sales	6/1–ongoing
Cut down on my living expenses	3/1–ongoing
(1) Give up my gym membership and start running every day	3/1–ongoing
(2) Don't buy any new clothes unless essential	3/1–ongoing
(3) Eat out at restaurants less often	3/1–ongoing
(4) make plans for a cheap vacation this year with a borrowed mountain cabin instead of planning an expensive vacation	4/1–4/30

Goals & Tasks	Scheduling
Free up 10–20 hours/week by cutting back paid employment and housework	3/1–ongoing
(1) get my husband and kids to do some extra household chores so I can paint on evenings and weekends, working up to 10 hours of painting time per week	3/1–ongoing
(2) go part-time with my job, cutting back at first to 30 hours per week, and use that time plus free time on evenings and weekends to paint, working up to 20 hours of painting time per week	6/1–ongoing
Make paintings that are exciting to me and attractive to potential collectors	4/1–ongoing
(1) begin making paintings that are fun and exciting to create	4/1–ongoing
(2) explore the idea of painting "home portraits"—portraits of people's homes—and experiment with other subjects that are interesting to me	5/1–ongoing
(3) take private lessons with a local painter to improve my skills and learn new techniques	5/1–7/31
(4) show my paintings to my husband and friends and get their feedback	6/1–ongoing

Goals & Tasks	Scheduling
Be my own dealer—rent a gallery space periodically and hold exhibits twice a year	8/1–ongoing
(1) Talk to Janie S. and other gallery owners about renting a gallery space periodically	6/1–7/30
(2) Hold a summer show at Janie S.'s (or someone else's) gallery	8/1–8/31
(3) Hold a second show near Christmas, either at a gallery or in my home	12/1–12/31
(4) If these shows are successful, continue to hold semiannual exhibitions of my own work	next year–ongoing
(5) If I find that I don't sell enough paintings this way, look into finding a gallery that might want to represent my work or join a cooperative gallery	next year
Develop a comprehensive marketing plan promoting my paintings to a wide range of local and national buyers	10/1–12/31
(1) Have a working lunch with my friend Rita J., who is a public relations and marketing consultant, and get her advice about how best to market my "home portraits" to local and national collectors. Ask her for ideas about marketing my work through local real estate firms, exhibiting in galleries and at home, and using Internet marketing, advertising, direct mail, etc.	10/1–10/31
(2) Offer Rita a painting in exchange for her developing a comprehensive public relations and marketing plan for me	10/1–11/31
(3) Pursue the public relations and marketing plan Rita develops for me, using it to reach a large and diverse clientele with my work	12/1–ongoing

Goals & Tasks	Scheduling
Make enough money from my painting to allow me to give up my real estate career and become a full-time artist	next year
(1) Using the strategies described in the previous two goals, sell 15 paintings a year at $2000 each to earn a base income of $30,000	next year
(2) Once I reach an annual income of $30,000 from my painting, give up my real estate job	next year
(3) Continue to sell more paintings, and as demand increases, raise my prices so that I can reach a target income of $50,000 from my artwork annually	year after that
Reward myself for my focus and hard work in this new career, and reward family members for their support	3/1–ongoing
(1) Create periodic rewards for myself like "feasts of the senses"—candlelight dinners with my husband, country picnics with family, solo visits to museum shows—that nurture my senses and stimulate my creativity	3/1–ongoing
(2) Be sure to take one family vacation each year, but cut expenses by driving and by borrowing friends' vacation homes; do the same for occasional solo getaways	3/1–ongoing
(3) Be sure to keep a balance between work and leisure, not forgetting to spend time relaxing with my family and friends, working in the garden, and just doing nothing	3/1–ongoing

Exercise: Putting it all down on paper

Following the instructions provided on the previous pages, write down your vision statement, goals, and tasks in the order they will need to be achieved using the format below. Leave the scheduling section blank until you complete the exercises in chapter 19.

Vision

_____

_____

_____

_____

_____

_____

_____

Goals & Tasks   Scheduling
[Goal]

_____   _____

_____   _____

[Tasks]

_____   _____

_____   _____

_____   _____

_____   _____

_____   _____

_____   _____

_____   _____

_____   _____

_____   _____

_____   _____

_____   _____

Exercise: Putting it all down on paper

Goals & Tasks
[Goal]   Scheduling

_____   _____

_____   _____

[Tasks]

_____   _____

_____   _____

_____   _____

_____   _____

_____   _____

_____   _____

_____   _____

_____   _____

_____   _____

_____   _____

[Goal]

_____   _____

_____   _____

[Tasks]

_____   _____

_____   _____

_____   _____

_____   _____

_____   _____

_____   _____

_____   _____

_____   _____

_____   _____

_____   _____

CHAPTER 19

How long will it take?

Scheduling Success

One of the most common mistakes that organizations make, once they have finished writing their plans for the future, is to stash them away in a filing cabinet and ignore them. They may have paid consultants thousands of dollars and spent long days in committee meetings in order to create their plans, but they don't use them once they are written. They go about their business as usual, wondering why they aren't getting any closer to their envisioned futures—all because they forgot to schedule change. Does this sound familiar? How often have you planned to take an important action that would improve your life, and then kept postponing it because you hadn't written it down in your calendar? Change is hard. Unless you translate your plan into specific actions that you remind yourself to complete on time, it is all too easy to settle for maintaining the status quo.

Fortunately, we live in an era of time management mania. Scheduling tools and techniques abound, and those of us who want to be more organized and purposeful about how we live our lives can easily make use of them. Most of us don't just carry pocket calendars, we haul around bulky life planners that help us schedule up to two or three years in advance, and down to fifteen-minute intervals. Computers (ranging from the hand-held to the desktop) have programs that help us to organize our activities in as much or as little detail as we choose. Libraries and bookstores are full of books that describe a full range of time management techniques.

This is great news for late bloomers. If you are one of those people who revel in the mechanics of time management, then you will find it fairly easy to plug your life-changing goals and tasks into the scheduling system of your choice. But even if you balk at so much structure, don't worry. You can fall back on old reliable tools like to-do lists and simple calendars to help you stay on track.

Even though I am a failure at most time management techniques (I tend to forget to consult my calendar, or else I write things in the wrong place), I have taught myself how to stay on track regarding goals and tasks that are important. After attending a time management course that didn't "take," and buying and discarding several different calendars, I finally developed a to-do list system that works for me. The single most valuable piece of information that I gained from my forays into time management philosophy was this: "You can plan the life you want to have and lead it." For late bloomers, this means that you *can* schedule change. Simply make an appointment with the life you want to lead and keep it.

If you are dedicated to seeing your vision for the future become a reality, you will find a planning system that works for you. Since there is no way to fully predict the external events or internal shifts that will occur down the road, it can be difficult—and even frustrating—to try to schedule your life accurately more than a few months ahead. But you can schedule three months' worth of activities pretty accurately. By doing this, you can focus your energy upon the present and immediate future, and stop worrying so much about what may or may not happen six months—or a year—from now. If you translate your list of goals and tasks into a simple schedule that will remind you of what you need to do next, it will prevent you from falling into patterns of procrastination, no matter how anxious, distracted, or discouraged you may become.

In the following exercise, you will develop a scheduling technique that will help you stay on track, and on time, with your personal or professional transformation. Development and adoption of this scheduling system may prove more essential to your ultimate success than any other tool or technique described in this book. So, no matter how averse you may be to calendars, or how good you think you are at planning your time, do not skip this practical step!

PLANNING EXERCISES

Exercise: Scheduling change

1. Begin by reading through the life plan you prepared in chapter 18. For each goal and task you have set, try to imagine how long it will take you to complete it: two weeks? three months? half a year? Write these time estimates in pencil underneath your goals and tasks (see the example provided at the end of this chapter). Some goals or tasks you have described, such as major shifts in atti-

tude or behavior, may take a lifetime to achieve. Beneath these, write "ongoing." Others may be one-time actions that may take as little time as an hour or a day to complete. Write "one-time" beneath these.

Once you have written down your time estimates, take time to reread them and revise them. Be sure to compensate for your known tendencies. If you tend to try to cram too much into too little time, add in a few extra weeks or months. If things never take as long as you think they will, subtract some time.

2. Next, write today's date next to your first goal under the Scheduling column (see example provided at the end of this chapter). Then draw a hyphen next to the date, and after it write the date that you anticipate completing all the tasks that support this goal. For example, if today is September 1, and you estimate that it will take three months to achieve all the related tasks, then write next to the goal: *September 1–November 30.* Do this for each task and each goal in your plan. If some goals or tasks can be started before others are completed, then allow the dates you write down to overlap. For example, if your first goal is "attend a creative writing program," and your second goal is "write a novel," these goals can occur in an overlapping time frame. While the creative writing program may take six months to complete, you can start writing your novel after a few months of course work. The time frame for your first goal might be September 1–March 31 and the time frame for your second goal, January 1–December 31.

3. If you like using a calendar, then write the goals and tasks that you need to achieve in the next three months on your calendar. Just remember to write in pencil, since things don't always happen in the amount of time we imagine. In

addition to scheduling specific one-time activities in your calendar, also consider blocking out time in advance for the elements you wish to integrate into your life on a regular basis. If you know you want to exercise three times a week, or find quiet time to write every morning, then schedule it in your calendar over the next three-month period. In this way, you will be less likely to give up that hour to some demand that comes out of the blue and threatens to throw you off track.

4. If you have trouble with calendars (as I do), but like to-do lists, then you might try another technique for planning your life in three-month increments. Create a quarterly to-do list that includes the goals and tasks that you have planned to achieve during that time period (see the sample quarterly and weekly to-do lists provided at the end of this chapter for help). At the beginning of each week, look at your quarterly list and create a weekly to-do list that includes the task(s) that you can reasonably achieve within that week. At this point, you may want to add extra details that you did not include in your plan, breaking down tasks into even smaller, easily achieved actions.

   As you complete each action on your list, cross it off. Start a new to-do list at the beginning of the next week, carrying over any items you didn't finish from last week's list and adding new ones that you select from the quarterly list. When you get to the last week of the three-month period, start a new quarterly to-do list that includes any items you didn't complete from the last quarter, as well as the next set of goals and tasks from your overall life plan.

Pick either of these techniques or use both in tandem. If you have another planning system that works for you, then adapt these ideas to your own system. What is most important is that you begin scheduling and enacting change on a daily or weekly basis. Nothing is more gratifying than the knowledge that you are translating your ideal vision about how you want to live your life into daily reality.

If unexpected events come up, you can simply reschedule the events in your calendar or to-do list. Life is full of things that we cannot accurately schedule or predict, whether illness, pregnancy, natural disasters, falling in love, an unexpected job offer, or sudden revelations. Faced with such situations, late bloomers need to be both stubborn and flexible. You need to learn when situations really do call for you to postpone or radically change your plans, and when they are mirages, hurdles, or irrelevant coincidences that should be dismissed so you can move right along as planned. The following chapter will provide some practical guidelines to help you deal with unexpected circumstances.

Exercise: Scheduling change

Goals and Tasks	Scheduling
Put myself and my calling as an artist first in my life	3/1–ongoing
(ongoing)	
(1) ask my husband to take on weekday breakfast preparation so I can have quiet time; get whole family to agree that I can have 1/2 hour quiet time in the guest room each day	3/1–ongoing
(ongoing)	
(2) begin each day with a period of prayer and meditation during which I focus my attention and spiritual resources on answering my calling as an artist	3/1–ongoing
(ongoing)	
(3) take at least one action every day that translates my calling into reality	3/1–ongoing
(ongoing)	
Make paintings that are exciting to me and attractive to potential collectors	4/1–ongoing
(ongoing)	
(1) begin making paintings that are fun and exciting to create	4/1–ongoing
(ongoing)	
(2) explore the idea of painting "home portraits"–portraits of people's homes–and experiment with other subjects that are interesting to me	5/1–ongoing
(ongoing)	
(3) take private lessons with a local painter to improve my skills and learn new techniques	5/1–7/31
(3 months)	
(4) show my paintings to my husband and friends and get their feedback	6/1–ongoing
(ongoing)	**289**

Quarterly To-Do List

March 1–May 31

___ Begin each day with a period of prayer and meditation during which I focus my attention and spiritual resources on answering my calling as an artist

___ Take at least one action every day that translates my calling into reality

___ Set up the guest room as my studio/meditation room

___ Figure out exactly how much money I need each month

___ Talk to my husband about ways we can cut back on our living expenses

___ Figure out how many hours I will need to work selling real estate to meet my reduced needs (talk to other part-time realtors, etc.)

___ Talk to my boss about going part-time with my real estate job

___ Get my husband and kids to do some extra household chores so I can paint on evenings and weekends

___ Schedule appointment(s) with my therapist to discuss people-pleasing

___ Schedule lunch appointments with friends who are artists

___ Start painting: complete at least three paintings

Weekly To-Do List

March 1–March 7

Begin each day with a period of prayer and meditation during which I focus my attention and spiritual resources on answering my calling as an artist

Take at least one action every day that translates my calling into reality

Set up the guest room as my studio/meditation room

Call therapist to schedule appointment

Call one artist friend to schedule a lunch date

CHAPTER 20

How do I stay on course?

Traveling Tips for the Pursuit of Happiness

I once heard a late bloomer describe the impatience she felt when she first embarked upon her process of life change. "I planted a seed," she said, "and when that seed sent up a tiny, pale-green shoot, instead of rejoicing my first thought was to stomp on it and yell, 'You're not big enough!'" This image always makes me laugh. Once late bloomers get started with life change, they can become incredibly impatient. Having waited so long to do what we want with our lives, we begin to rush through the process of our transformation. As a result, we tend to forget to experience the pleasure of the journey.

Take a deep breath and relax. You have already begun to change your life. You have allowed yourself to envision in enticing detail the life you want to live. You have your strategic plan in hand to direct you toward that life. You have made an appointment with yourself to begin that journey in the immediate future, and you have created a schedule to help you stay on track and on time. Here are a few traveling tips to help you enjoy your trip and deal with the unexpected chances and changes you may encounter along the way.

Measure your progress

Once you begin following your plan, you must make a commitment to experience the process of your transformation with as much joy and excitement as your arrival at the ultimate destination. You can do this by looking for small signs of progress every day: the actions you take, the attitudes you adopt, *and* the results you get. These may not always be tangible, measurable results, like new income, public acclaim, or even outside recognition. They may be simple gifts, such as a sense of peace and serenity, a surge of energy, or an empowering purposefulness—the realization that you are living your life, for that moment or that day, the way you most want to, not just the way you happen to.

Some late bloomers keep journals in which they maintain a personal travel log, noting their progress, their experiences, and their emotions on a regular basis. Others make a habit of setting aside a few moments each day to check in with themselves (or a higher power) to give thanks for the gifts of the day, to seek strength for the challenges that face them, and to feel the transforming power that lies within, and around, them. Some late bloomers use this time to visualize the life they wish to move toward, in order to strengthen and encourage themselves as they travel forward. Others simply focus their energies upon the present, clarifying their vision of the work that needs to be done that day, and locating the source of energy they will need. Journal-writing, prayer, and meditation are all disciplines that can help you stay calm, positive, and centered as you undergo transformations that might otherwise seem quite disorienting.

Celebrate yourself

Celebration is a very important discipline for late bloomers to adopt. You need to find creative ways to recognize your progress, to reward yourself, and to honor your achievements. When an important task is completed, or a goal is met, don't just cross it off your calendar or to-do list. Mark these achievements with some tangible action. Perhaps you can give yourself a gift, whether it be a delightfully frivolous one (like a manicure or a small shopping spree), or something downright practical (like a new box of your favorite pens). Or perhaps your celebration might involve a special activity that gives you pleasure or reinforces the identity you have chosen to express in your new life or work: a gourmet meal with a loved one or mentor, a visit to a museum, or a trip to the beach. The gesture can be as small as buying yourself some flowers or as grand as a week-long vacation that is well-deserved. However you choose to mark your achievements, make a habit of honoring them throughout your transformation.

Create community

It can be very productive to create a community of people who know about your process of transformation, who share in your excitement, who encourage you when the going is slow, and who celebrate your achievements. Some late bloomers enlist therapists or other kinds of counselors to support their process of change. Others create communities that include their spouses, friends, and mentors. I have a monthly lunch date with a group of friends who are all devoted to living full and satisfying lives. We gather to applaud each other's achievements, air our frustrations, and cheer one another on. Another late bloomer I know has a virtual support group with which she corresponds via e-mail, announcing her progress on challenging life goals, expressing her thanks for their support, and soliciting their words of encouragement. Internet chat rooms provide another form of virtual community for late bloomers who share common challenges or goals.

Handling setbacks

All of the above techniques can help you to cope when you run into major challenges or obstacles along your way—as you inevitably will. You have done your best to predict the challenges you might encounter and to plan creative strategies to deal with them. Yet no amount of planning can fully prepare you for the experience of working through these challenges in real life. There may be times when the real world simply refuses to cooperate with your plans, sending far more resistance or rejection your way than you expected. You may also find that internal roadblocks crop up—perhaps old fears masquerading as reasonable doubts, anxiety, pessimism, depression, addictions you thought you had learned to deal with, and so on. The following techniques suggest a few different ways that you can handle such persistent challenges without turning around and going back.

The first thing that you must do is to accept challenges, and the hard work associated with overcoming them, as an inescapable aspect of life change. You are going to counteract years of momentum, peel back layers of assumed identities, dismantle expectations that others have about you and you have about yourself, and put a new life together, one piece at a time. This is work. But it is not thankless grunt work—no, the rewards of being true to yourself and your callings will come forth to meet you as soon as you reach out for them. For that reason, you need to approach your transformation with an attitude of optimism. Whether or not you are a natural optimist, you need to assume the discipline of positive thinking. You will quickly discover that optimism, like celebration, is not a painful discipline, and practicing either brings immediate rewards.

Choosing optimism

Instead of allowing yourself to be utterly demoralized or discouraged by temporary setbacks like rejection or resistance, you need to translate your initial response of frustration into new energy. React creatively. One way to do this is to look for the silver lining in *every* cloud. For example, one of my biggest goals was to get published. When I got my first rejection letter, after a few crestfallen moments I realized that this was actually an accomplishment that needed to be celebrated. I couldn't have received a rejection letter if I hadn't actually written something and submitted it to a publisher. This rejection letter was actually an affirmation that I was actively engaged in the process of becoming published. Any published writer will admit that his or her career began with rejection. For late bloomers, most setbacks are not just temporary impediments to success, they are also, paradoxically, indications of progress.

Other setbacks that may be familiar to you are being turned down for a coveted job, being rejected by the school of your choice, failing an entrance exam, or having a relationship fall short of your expectations. One late bloomer I know had her heart set upon attending graduate school at an Ivy League university on the East Coast. Unfortunately, her applications were rejected by the Ivy Leagues to which she applied, and she had no choice but to attend her backup school in California. Once she relocated to the West Coast and began to tap into its healthy, outdoor lifestyle, she began to rekindle her childhood love of hiking and backpacking. This unexpected gift was the direct result of the rejection she had encountered earlier and, in retrospect, she was able to recognize that this setback was a step toward the life she wanted to lead. Of course, it is always much easier to make these attitude adjustments retroactively. But by adopting the discipline of optimism, you can try to find the yes hidden inside each no as soon as you encounter it.

Cultivating perseverance

Whether you can find a silver lining in every cloud or not, you *can* decide that you won't let stormy weather stop you from moving forward. I have always loved the steely determination expressed by the U.S. Postal Service's unofficial motto: "Neither snow nor rain nor heat nor gloom of night stays these couriers from the swift completion of their appointed rounds." The English, forever coping with rain and fog and seeping dampness, more lightheartedly commit to "weather the weather, whatever the weather, whether we like it or not." Both mottoes apply to late bloomers. Things may not always go your way, but you can keep going your way just the same. If it is storming out, then you simply need to get an umbrella.

Sometimes, all you need to do is to create a new coping mechanism or a strategy that will allow you to stay on course.

One late-blooming friend adopted a strategy that required him to take a positive action within forty-eight hours of any setback he encountered. This strategy, which I highly recommend to other late bloomers, prevents him from dwelling too long on rejection or failure and keeps him from spiraling down into a pit of despair.

I am sure you know how tempting it is to allow setbacks, however large or small, to trigger your pessimism or low self-esteem, and to reactivate your fear that fate will somehow frustrate or shortchange you every step of the way.

It is natural to succumb to these feelings from time to time. But by taking actions that demonstrate hope instead of despair and favor progress over retreat, you can counteract your feelings of hopelessness and frustration while improving the odds of reaching the goals you have set. Sometimes, success is simply a numbers game. You have to try a certain number of times before you can succeed.

Changing plans

If, after adopting these disciplines, you still find that certain external events threaten to slow your progress significantly (or actually block your way to the desired destination), then you may need to rewrite a portion of your plan. Use the exercises provided for identifying challenges and corresponding goals and tasks to create alternative strategies whenever you need to. Every plan for life change involves some delays and detours. Some plans will just require more than others.

If persistent efforts demonstrate that your original vision is truly inaccessible, then you need to be willing to create a new, more accessible vision for your future and revise your plan accordingly. In chapter 2, you defined what success meant to you *before* you created the detailed vision of the future you hoped to achieve. Even if you need to shift and refocus some of the details of this vision, you will probably find that the elements of success you defined can remain constant. For example, Jerri, the late-blooming poetry therapist, knew that success, for her, meant living with poetry as an active part of her daily life. For a while, she believed that this would be achieved by pursuing a graduate degree in creative writing from a prestigious university. When the school turned her down, she was able to revise her vision for the future, shifting direction toward a degree in poetry therapy, without giving up her commitment to engaging daily with poetry.

Sometimes, late bloomers find that detours are necessitated not by external resistance or roadblocks, but by internal shifts. Perhaps you started out in one direction, with a certain destination in mind, and realized along the way that you no longer want to travel in that direction. You may have gained some new information about the destination toward which you are traveling, or some new insights about yourself, which point to an alternate destination.

If you feel a persistent desire to change direction, you should not ignore it. Persistent is the key word, however, because late bloomers often experience temporary desires to jump ship, swim to shore, or try a new tack. These often turn out to be false alarms—moments of anxiety or unconscious delaying tactics. I recommend that you wait at least a month or more before deciding to change your course radically. If, however, you continue to feel that you want to redirect your journey, then you should do so, rewriting your plan to describe a different course of action.

Living in the moment

Whatever you do along the way, whether you follow your plan to the letter or radically revise it as you travel along, be sure not to postpone happiness any longer. There is an adage that hikers employ that reminds them to *stop, look, listen, and learn* as they follow mountain trails. Otherwise, they are apt to rush up hills or down into valleys, reaching the end of the trail breathless, exhausted, and unaware of the many unexpected pleasures that unfolded along the way. Anyone who has enacted life change will tell you that the destination itself is usually only another rest stop. Once it is reached, the road keeps winding on through different terrain. The purpose of your traveling is not to rush toward a finite state of happiness, but rather to escape from dead ends of dissatisfaction by actively engaging in the pursuit of happiness.

The moment you turned your gaze inward, asking yourself hard questions and listening carefully to the answers, you demonstrated a whole new level of courage and dedication to the quality of your life. Once you translated this information into a written plan of action and began to follow it, you took an extraordinary leap of faith. By harnessing the power of courage, devotion, and faith, mixed with common sense and unconventional wisdom, you connected with powerful and inspiring sources of energy. This energy will speed you along your path of transformation, it will also fill each hour of your journey with joy. Don't forget to feel your bliss while you follow it!

American poet Walt Whitman, a late bloomer who failed at many jobs before he published the first edition of his magnum opus, *Leaves of Grass,* at the age of 36, described the joy of journeying hopefully into life in his poem "Song of the Open Road." His words serve as both a description of this lifelong journey and a parting benediction for you as you prepare to set off on your adventure into the life well lived.

From this hour I ordain myself loos'd of limits and
    imaginary lines,
Going where I list, my own master total and absolute,
Listening to others, considering well what they say,
Pausing, searching, receiving, contemplating,
Gently, but with undeniable will, divesting myself of the
    holds that would hold me.

I inhale great draughts of space,
The east and the west are mine, and the north and the
    south are mine.

I am larger, better than I thought,
I did not know I held so much goodness.

All seems beautiful to me,
I can repeat over to men and women, You have done such
'   *good to me I would do the same to you,*
I will recruit for myself and you as I go,
I will scatter myself among men and women as I go,
I will toss a new gladness and roughness among them,
Whoever denies me it shall not trouble me,
Whoever accepts me he or she shall be blessed and shall
    bless me.

Go now! And enjoy your trip.

Index

Printed in the United States
862500001B